staying mum

staying mum

What your MUM forgot to tell you and your BEST FRIENDS never dared!

Mara Lee

For my family, but especially for Birdy

First published 2010 by Wrightbooks
an imprint of John Wiley & Sons Australia, Ltd
42 McDougall Street, Milton Qld 4064

Office also in Melbourne

Typeset in Berkley LT 11.3/14pt

© Mara Lee 2010

The moral rights of the author have been asserted

National Library of Australia Cataloguing-in-Publication data:

Author:	Lee, Mara.
Title:	Staying mum: what your mum forgot to tell you and your best friends never dared! / Mara Lee.
Edition:	Revised ed.
ISBN:	9781742169941 (pbk.)
Notes:	Includes index.
Subjects:	Infants—Care.
Dewey Number:	649.122

Cover design by Xou Creative

Printed in Australia by McPherson's Printing Group

10 9 8 7 6 5 4 3 2 1

Disclaimer
The material in this publication is of the nature of general comment only, and does not represent professional advice. It is not intended to provide specific guidance for particular circumstances and it should not be relied on as the basis for any decision to take action or not take action on any matter which it covers. Readers should obtain professional advice where appropriate, before making any such decision. To the maximum extent permitted by law, the author and publisher disclaim all responsibility and liability to any person, arising directly or indirectly from any person taking or not taking action based upon the information in this publication.

Contents

About the author

Widely considered to be one of Australia's favourite parenting experts, Mara Lee is a journalist, author, TV personality, wife, mother of two and the editor of Australia's favourite parenting magazine, *Practical Parenting*.

Mara completed her communications degree at Macquarie University, after which she worked at Reed Business Information as a journalist. She joined *Bride to Be* magazine in 1998, where she quickly earned her stripes and became the editor. In 2000, Mara was appointed editor of *Practical Parenting*. She was the parenting presenter on *Mornings with Kerri-Anne* for many years, and now appears regularly as a parenting commentator on *Sunrise* and *The Morning Show*.

Her greatest achievement, however, is being a devoted mum of two gorgeous children, now aged 11 and nine.

Mara lives in Sydney with her husband Tony (aka Bing), daughter Jayna (aka Jaybird) and son, the incredibly super Cooper.

Acknowledgements

Heartfelt thanks to all the fabulous people who helped to deliver this baby: Jane Ogilvie, for conceiving the idea and for nurturing both the book and its author throughout the gestational period; Mary Masters, for breathing new life into the project; and editors Cathy Proctor and Ilaria Walker, for taking such tender loving care with the manuscript.

And enormous gratitude to my family, who were drawn into the labour ward with me whether they liked it or not. To Bing, my life support system (and sometimes anaesthetist!). To Jaybird, who may not have fitted into my life, but who certainly made it better. To Super Cooper, who fitted in a little easier, but that was probably because he had a tendency to bash things into shape. And to Mum and Dad, who have always been my role models even though it isn't always obvious.

Chapter 1

Honey, *it's time!*

Birth

The baby was delivered and, miraculously, there had been no pain. Mum handed me my newborn, all wrapped up in schmaltzy baby paper — but just as I was about to peer between its legs to discover if we qualified for a blue or pink Bonds jumpsuit, I felt a dull ache in my stomach.

Then I woke up. It was, literally, the wee hours of Wednesday morning.

Bugger. Bump still there, bigger than ever. Baby still head-butting my bladder and, speaking of that poor excuse for a body part, I need to go. Again. Well, it *has* been three hours since my last pee.

The Big Guy's side of the bed visibly drops as I success-fully execute my most complicated move of the day — a combination of rolling, clawing and heaving myself out of bed — but he doesn't wake. Then again, the man has slept through nine months of nocturnal tossing and turning and trips to the toilet, so why should tonight be any different?

I've almost reached the throne, wondering if I'm insane for even thinking about going to work today given that I'm nine months pregnant and feeling like I'm about to get my period, when I realise that my knickers are wet. Actually, I'm soaked from the groin down. Great. Now I'm fat, crazy and incontinent. Then it dawns: this would be my waters — only they don't seem to be breaking, as such. More like I'm slowly peeing my pants, to be brutally honest.

When your waters break

Your unborn baby floats around inside a protective membrane filled with amniotic fluid. At some point before or even during labour, the sac may rupture. This is referred to as your 'waters breaking'. You may feel a big gush of liquid, a small trickle or a continuous leak.

If your waters break before you start having regular strong contractions, you will need to contact your midwife or obstetrician to let them know what's happened. You will probably be asked to go straight to hospital, and you may end up being induced if labour doesn't start within 24 hours as there is a risk of infection once the sac has ruptured.

If your waters don't break naturally, your carer may decide to do this manually, once you are in hospital, in order to speed up or induce your labour. In some cases, babies are born in nature's packaging with the membrane intact. This is known as being 'born in the caul'.

I guess I won't be going in to work today after all. For once, the deadline will have to wait. Probably a tad early at 3 am to call in sick — or, more specifically, dilating — so better call the hospital instead. Better call my mum, just because it will make the whole 'I'm about to have a baby' thing seem more real. Better tell the Big Guy he's soon to be a dad.

Pickle me amniotic fluid

Contrary to folklore, you probably won't make an enormous puddle if your waters break in public. So no need to carry a jar of pickled onions in your handbag to smash 'just in case'. If you're worried about getting caught short, wear a maternity pad when you go out instead.

An hour later at 4 am, I am sitting on a pile of towels in the car next to the Big Guy, feeling confident about my imminent labour. I am prepared, after all, with the essentials: a CD player and a pile of CDs. All the books I've read recommend soothing music and dim lights to create our preferred ambiance, and like the enthusiastic first timers that we are, we buy the whole deal and throw in an aromatherapy candle for good measure. We've got jazz, rainforest sounds and a rogue Cold Chisel compilation that the Big Guy snuck in when he thought I wasn't looking. As if labour is going to distract me enough to allow him to play that! Ah well, who cares? We're on our way to the hospital, thrilled that the midwives told me I was to come straight in, and that I won't be going home until I have my baby. The Big Guy keeps looking over at me, patting my thigh and grinning like the Cheshire Cat. 'We're having a baby, we're having a baby', we chant smugly. This is a piece of cake. And just like my dream, there's no pain.

I become more than a bit disappointed to discover that the reason for the lack of pain is the lack of established labour. At hospital, I'm monitored for an hour or so before being tucked up in bed. The plan is to wait for labour to start spontaneously within 24 hours, or be induced if it doesn't. It's now 5 am. Like there's any chance of sleep. The Big Guy is urged to go home and I suddenly feel weepy. I want him here. I want the baby. I want — dare I say it — to be in labour.

Bless his cotton jocks, the Big Guy returns after breakfast to mooch around with me. We decide to do everything we can to bring on labour naturally, but the midwives flatly refuse to allow us to practise what they preach in antenatal classes: hot curries, hot baths and hot sex to get things going. It's a shared ward, after all. Walking around the hospital grounds, however, is completely acceptable so we set off at a cracking pace, me leaking amniotic fluid with every step. The Big Guy starts making jokes concerning my thighs and 'slippery when wet' signs, which are funny for about the first hour, but just annoying after that. By early afternoon, after what feels like our millionth lap around the hospital, his enthusiasm starts to wane.

Conversation has become nonexistent, except for the Big Guy's gentle pleading for me to give it a rest. 'Sorry mate,' I mutter through gritted teeth, 'no can do'. Knowing full well that I won't stop until I have my own way, he groans inwardly but humours me outwardly by taking my hand and steering me towards a new walking route. Our perseverance pays off, and 10 minutes later I am rewarded with my first contraction, which feels like someone is firmly squeezing my insides.

We race back inside to tell the midwives about this monumental development, expecting them to pounce on the news, steer me into the labour ward and extract the baby effortlessly in the next half hour or so. Nope, they shoo me away and tell me to come back when I have something they can work with. I guess being constantly exposed to the blessed miracle of birth, day in and day out, can make one somewhat blasé. And crusty. I turn on my soggy heels and brace myself for more laps.

Signs that labour is looming

There are many different ways your body signals to you that labour is imminent and some will present hours, days or even weeks before the real action begins. You may register one, several or none of these pre-labour signs before you begin having the strong, frequent and increasingly more painful contractions of full-blown labour. 'Pre-labour', as these early signs are called, is more common with first babies and typical symptoms include:

* little niggles such as backache or period-like pains

* mild contractions, widely or irregularly spaced

* nausea, vomiting or diarrhoea

* finding a glob of mucous in your knickers (commonly referred to as having a 'show')

* waters breaking

* feeling a little unwell, or just a bit 'off'

* experiencing an insatiable urge to clean the house/baby's room/kitchen/skirting boards like you've never cleaned before!

Women who race off to hospital during pre-labour often find they are sent home again to wait for true labour to begin. This can be disappointing and frustrating, but it's also a golden opportunity to conserve your energy and rest up for the big event that's just around the corner.

By Wednesday evening, contractions are still only 30 minutes apart and, apparently, too pathetic to warrant attention — so the midwives bully the Big Guy out the door again, telling him to go home and get some sleep because labour and our baby won't be making an appearance tonight. I'm even tearier than ever and ache to feel the pain of real labour.

At 9 pm I turn off my light and try to sleep, but I can't because suddenly I'm moaning. Did I say I ached for the pain of labour? What an idiot. Send the godforsaken contractions away and bring me the Big Guy. A shot of pethidine and a midwife — crusty or otherwise — would also go down well at this particular point in time, despite the fact that I had categorically vetoed pethidine in the birth plan I never got around to writing. Just as well, I thought ruefully, as I presented my backside for the nurse and her needle full of narcotics.

Contraction action

Contractions play an important role in labour: they coax your cervix to open (dilate) to 10 centimetres wide, so that the second stage of labour — pushing — can begin.

Contractions may build up from weak (like period pain) to strong (you can't move during one) over a period of hours or days, or they may hit suddenly with little build-up or warning. If you can still talk through your contractions, chances are you are still in pre-labour.

True labour is when your contractions are two to four minutes apart and last for around 45 to 60 seconds — you time them by counting the minutes between the beginning of one

At some ungodly hour on Thursday morning, a good 24 hours after my waters broke, I decide that's it. I'm going. Finito. You can take your freakin' heart monitor and surgical gloves and stick them somewhere else, because I don't want to play this game anymore. The pethidine didn't seem to make a jot of difference, except to make me feel guilty that I had the stupid drug in the first place! I've been in the first stage of labour for six hours and dilation is two-thirds of zip. Three centimetres in six hours just doesn't make the grade. Too bad, so sad, I'll be off then. Except I can't leave.

Plans? What plans?

Writing a birth plan is a great idea in theory. It encourages you to form an opinion on issues such as which pain relief and medical interventions you may or may not want to use during labour. But be prepared to be flexible. You may be advised to take a different path depending on how your labour progresses.

I can barely bring myself to move from the bed, despite the fact that I assured myself I was going to have an active contraction and the beginning of the next one.

It's not uncommon for women to turn up on the maternity ward's doorstep after a few hours of mild contractions at home, only to have those contractions fade away to almost nothing. The theory is that hospital makes some women feel a little nervous or tense, and the resulting adrenalin surge temporarily suppresses the contractions that brought them there in the first place. Very strong established contractions, on the other hand, are unlikely to slow down by a change of scenery. As a result, most midwives advise staying at home for as long as possible, and to wait until you've moved into established labour before setting off for hospital.

labour and let gravity help me drop my bundle. In fact, I can't even open my mouth to do any more than emit eerie cow-like noises that vary in intensity as each contraction starts, peaks and then ends. I'm not a pretty sight and I don't give a damn. My back kills and the contractions send me feral. The baby is grinding deep down into my pelvis and the stubborn thing won't come out.

I'm put on a drip to help induce stronger contractions, because at the rate I'm going—one centimetre every two hours—it feels like everyone in the room could be spending my first Mother's Day together. And it's only March. One of the midwives tells me that this baby will be born before her shift ends, which is in three hours. I desperately want to believe her, but by now I am not even aware that I am having a baby. I'm just having pain—and lots of it.

The Big Guy is doing his best to help, but there's nothing the poor sod can do. After a well-meaning (but let's face it, fairly useless) attempt to comfort me with a solid couple of hours of brow wiping, he retires to an armchair to stare at me helplessly while I continue to writhe around dramatically, letting everyone in on my pain. Neither of us has slept since Tuesday night and we are both tragic. Of course, I'm more tragic than he is, but if I had any capacity for intelligent thought I would probably feel a little sorry for him, too, because he has to watch me go through this—and that must be its own unique form of torture.

The CDs lie on a side bench, completely redundant. Music as pain relief? What on earth were we thinking?

Liar midwife has finished her shift and the baby is still nowhere in sight. The drip is now cranked up to maximum, so the contractions pound away mercilessly. There is no beginning, peak and end to each gut-wrenching squeeze: I'm now permanently peaking. Somehow, in the whole surreal, confusing, foggy experience, someone discovers that the baby is facing the wrong way, which explains why this labour has been so, well, laborious. The diagnosis may well have come from the cleaner—I'm sure she was among the cast of thousands in there having a look at one stage.

Finally my cervix reaches the magical 10 centimetres-wide mark, and I'm given the nod to bear down and evict my little wombmate. Only the stubborn thing is not so little, and refuses to budge—despite two solid hours of pushing until I swear my eyeballs will pop. And so the obstetrician is summoned to put an end to this seemingly never-ending labour.

A cut below

An episiotomy can be the stuff of nightmares—until you have one, that is. You really won't feel a thing when it actually happens, as you are given a numbing anaesthetic beforehand. Plus, it will help your baby be born faster. Trust me, it's all good.

I'd like to be able to say I had a natural birth, but I'm not quite sure that I qualify. Try as I may, I can't see anything natural about pushing a four-kilogram football with arms, legs and a head out of an opening that's used to dealing with inches. And there is definitely nothing natural about enduring 17 hours of pain, being drip-fed a hormonal cocktail to induce my wrong-way-around baby, a cut to my nether regions, a vacuum extraction and half an hour of intimate repairs afterwards.

There is an upside to the whole ordeal, of course — I can now go out and buy a pink Bonds jumpsuit. Through hormonally charged tears of relief I register that my daughter is smeared with blood and gunk, sporting a mullet and more than vaguely reminiscent of the Big Guy's hairy Uncle Otto. We call her Xena, the name we have been quietly cooing into my belly for the last three months. Naturally, she is the most divine thing I have ever seen.

When Mother Nature needs a helping hand

At some point during your labour, your carer may feel that you need some medical assistance to keep you and your baby safe. It may be that your labour isn't progressing or your baby is in a less-favourable position, stuck, or beginning to show signs of distress. These procedures include:

- *induction*. Methods include prostaglandin gel inserted into the vagina (this is usually the first attempt to bring on labour when a baby is overdue), an intravenous drip of syntocinon (often used after the gel hasn't had an effect, or to kickstart contractions that have slowed down or stopped) or the artificial rupture of membranes (when your midwife or obstetrician breaks your waters).

- *ventouse suction cup*. A rubber cap is placed on your unborn baby's head, creating a vacuum. Your carer pulls on the tube attached to the cap as you push your baby out.

- *forceps*. These look like oversized salad servers, and are inserted into your vagina to grip onto your baby and help pull him or her out as you push.

- *episiotomy.* This is a cut into the area between your vagina and anus to make more room for the baby to come out.

- *caesarean section.* This is where your baby is removed from your womb via abdominal surgery. A caesarean performed before the onset of labour is called an elective caesarean, but one performed during labour is called an emergency caesarean.

Chapter 2

From me *to mum*

Day 0: immediately after birth

I let the steady stream of water pound down on me, my aching body strangely soothed by taking another beating—albeit a much more gentle one than it had just endured in the delivery suite. Long strands of hair swept into my eyes and onto my face but I couldn't be bothered pushing them back. Didn't have the strength to, in fact. Standing under that shower, chin to chest, arms hanging limply at my side with the water washing the blood, sweat and tears from Xena's birth off my body was about as much as I could manage.

It was hard to believe that less than an hour ago I had been in the throes of hell. Even harder to believe that the person who gave birth to Xena was me. Had I really anchored myself to that bed, sucking ferociously on the gas as each contraction gained momentum? Was that really my voice, sobbing that I couldn't do it anymore, and then bellowing angrily with every push? Were those really my legs in (cringe!) stirrups as the obstetrician helped end the whole ordeal with an episiotomy? It was only the tightness of the newly stitched seam in the area between my backside and frontside that reassured me of my involvement in a birth that seemed like it had happened to someone else.

You did it, girl! I congratulated myself in sheer amazement. No more worrying about the birth, no more imagining how I would cope with the pain. I had coped and, in doing so, had conquered my fear. I had grown a baby and pushed it out of my body. Was there anything I couldn't do? Come to think of it, I couldn't stand up in the shower any longer, even though it was doing such a fabulous job on the neck, shoulder and upper arm muscles I had unwittingly strained during the exhausting pushing stage. Feeling weak and shaky after

Caring for your episiotomy

You may feel a little uncomfortable and conscious of your stitches following an episiotomy, but they won't take long to heal completely if you take a little care to keep your bits clean and dry. Here's how:

- Pat the area (don't rub) with clean toilet paper after number ones. You can even keep a jug of clean water by the loo to pour over your stitches when you use the toilet. Then pat dry.

- Use a clean towel to dab at the area after showering, or even use a hairdryer to dry off down there for the first few days — seriously!

several minutes on my feet, I figured it was time to get myself back on dry ground, preferably in a reclined position.

I staggered out of the recess and attempted to dry myself discreetly. White towels in a maternity ward? It just didn't make sense. What happened next also made no sense at all.

Reaching into my meticulously packed hospital bag filled with brand-new pyjamas and the first pair of slippers I'd owned since I was 10, I pulled out a pair of cargos I had brought in for my hospital stay. They made it all the way up to my thighs. What the?

I had assumed—apparently rather foolishly—that baby out meant stomach back in, and it had never occurred to

Mummy's first poop

Number twos after an episiotomy can feel a bit scary, as naturally you worry about tearing the stitches when you strain. You can help ease the pressure by resting your feet on a low stool (no pun intended!) so your knees are higher than your lap. Holding a wad of clean toilet paper against your stitches when you go can also help.

- Dab on some witch hazel after showering to help the wound heal.
- Always wipe downwards and away from your stitches after number twos. Again, pouring clean water over your bits and then patting dry can help you feel clean without harming your repairs.

Within a week or two the stitches will dissolve on their accord. If at any time you notice more pain, or a suspicious smell or discharge, see your GP or carer immediately to rule out infection.

me to pack maternity clothes for after the birth. But no matter how many times I stretched out the waist band of my pre-baby pants across my own stretched-out (and nonexistent) waist, it was pretty clear that wearing non-maternity pants was just a pipe dream. The awful reality was that I still looked five months pregnant, except my bump was now spongy and soggy instead of tight and round. To make matters worse, the only maternity duds I had with me were those I had worn to hospital on the morning my waters broke—and I was just so over the whole amniotic fluid thing.

Debriefing after birth

It's quite normal to feel a bit shell-shocked after the birth, especially if your labour spiralled into unfamiliar or frightening territory, or ended in an unplanned caesarean. Ask your midwife or obstetrician to explain the hows, whens and whys of your labour and birth to help you make sense of what happened and why, and move forward with a positive mindset.

Longing for my old discreet pot-belly—if only I had known that compared with this, it had almost been flat!—I reluctantly ditched the nowhere-near-fitting cargos for my amniotic-fluid-soaked pants, the only item of clothing that could comfortably accommodate the saggy baggy elephant skin that hung like a deflated balloon where my once glorious bump had been. Then I made a mental note to ask the Big Guy to bring in some more appropriate clothes when he came back the next day, and to have a quiet word to his mum about those 'step-ins' she swore by. There was a time I sniggered about big lady underpants that pulled in slothful tummies, but suddenly I understood their reason for being. Heck, I may even have a need for them, depending on how long it took me to move this thing.

Your body after birth

It took nine months and, on average, a 10 to 13 kilogram gain to make your beautiful baby and it can take just as long (or even longer) for your body to recover from all this activity and growth. In fact some experts believe it takes anywhere between six and 12 months for your body to totally recover from pregnancy, labour and birth. Some of the common after-effects include:

- *saggy tummy and a thicker waistline.* Sadly, abdominal exercises are the only sure-fire way to regain muscle tone.

- *stretchmarks around your hips, thighs, tummy, breasts or bottom.* These fade from purply red lines to silvery streaks in time. You can use creams and oils to speed up the recovery process, although the efficacy of these types of products is debatable.

- *pimples.* As your hormones continue to run rampant after birth, you may suffer from breakouts. Stock up on face wash and zit blitzer and drink tons of water.

- *bigger feet.* Some women find they go up half or a whole shoe size after having a baby, possibly due to weight gain and fluid retention, not because their feet grow in length.

- *haemorrhoids.* These are caused by pregnancy or the pushing stage. Avoid constipation (which exacerbates the condition) by keeping up your fibre and fluid intake, and ask your GP to prescribe a suitable cream.

Pale-faced, still shaking, but finally dressed, I limped out to meet up with the midwife who ushered me into a wheelchair and rolled me back to my family in the maternity ward. The Big Guy looked up as I entered the room. Cradling little Xena in his big blokey arms he looked fit to burst. His face said it all: 'Look what we made. She's ours'. My heart skipped a beat, and I swear I couldn't have been any prouder at that moment had my wheelchair been a chariot and the whopping great maternity pad I was sitting on been a throne. Gingerly I eased my battered bits down onto the bed and reached out for my girl. The Big Guy squeezed onto the bed with us, firmly glued to my side. The three of us snuggled up in a dreamy euphoria, Xena's head resting on the soft spot between my neck and shoulder and her body moulded into mine as if it were custom-made for her. Whispering how beautiful she was, how clever we were, how amazing life is, we waited for our first visitors to arrive.

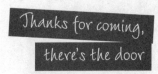

Thanks for coming, there's the door

Visitors mean well, but at times you may prefer to be alone with your baby, especially if you're feeling frazzled, tired or reluctant to breastfeed with an audience. Feel free to use 'midwives orders to rest' to deter drop-ins and switch your phones off whenever you need an hour or two of peace.

Day 1

The Big Guy spent his time after Xena's birth zipping back and forth between the hospital and his office, tying up loose ends at work so he could officially begin his two weeks of leave to coincide with our arrival home. Every time he poked his grinning noggin around the doorway my spirits soared, not least because sharing a room with other new mums hadn't been the social, mutually backslapping experience I had hoped it would be. Even though the midwives flung back the curtains around our beds at every opportunity and verbally encouraged my room-mates and I to create some sort of sisterhood, we pretty much ignored each other. Goodness knows I tried my hardest to ignore their babies crying on the occasions when mine slept. At most we exchanged a shy smile and the odd grimace before we plunged back into our own worlds.

When I told the Big Guy how grateful I was for his company, he just looked at me in amused disbelief: 'Like I could stay away, you crazy mumma'. For the umpteenth time in my life I thanked my lucky stars for having found this adorable guy. We had only been separated for two nights but I missed him terribly. We'd shared so many milestones that it felt strange to have arrived at this significant point in our lives and not be able to share every moment.

I reasoned that going home together would restore a sense of normality.

Secret women's business

You may have heard horror stories about mums who leak when they laugh, cough, sneeze or suddenly have to dash after a runaway toddler. Don't let this happen to you!

These 'leaks' occur because your pelvic floor (the muscles between your vagina and your anus) has been weakened during pregnancy and birth. It might need a bit of boot camp to toughen up again. Pelvic floor exercises (also known as Kegel exercises) are simple and discreet—no-one can tell when you're doing them. To do these exercises, pull up all the muscles in the area as if you are pretending to stop a wee midstream. Now hold for 10 seconds. Do 10 repetitions, at least three times a day.

The hardest part of the exercises is actually remembering to do your daily quota. To remind yourself to do them, it's a good idea to link your pelvic floor exercises with a regular daily activity, such as nappy change time or a trip to the loo. You can start immediately after the birth, although you may be a little numb and unable to feel much going on down there for the first few days. Continue for as long as you feel the need—this may be months or even years, especially if you are planning to have more babies.

I also suspected that I would feel more like myself when I could stop showing my intimate bits to the entire hospital. Alas, it wasn't to be. The slight yellow tinge to Xena's skin kept us anchored firmly to the maternity ward for at least three or four more days, until the paediatrician was satisfied her condition had improved. So twice a day I was obliged to assume 'the position'. Think of a chicken lying on its side, waiting to be stuffed, and you're on the right track. Apparently the destruction site was healing, and things were looking pretty spiffy down there—which was just great, but also a complete and utter waste given that no man would ever go there again if I had any say in the matter. I could only hope that the Big Guy would accept my sincere apologies for any inconvenience caused.

The other previously private parts of my body to gain an unprecedented amount of attention were, of course, my bosoms. From the moment Xena's cord was cut, my bosoms became public property—as demonstrated by the midwife who started kneading my flesh into mouth-sized morsels for my minutes-old daughter while I lay on the delivery bed, shaking with the aftershock of labour. Much to my surprise, when Xena refused to take the bait, the midwife then proceeded to physically milk me. The amount of time spent scrounging for milk that hadn't 'come in yet' amazed me. So did the fact that a few drops of creamy goo from my boobs constituted a feed. A feed, in my eyes, was a bowl of pasta, side salad and a nice drop of vino to wash it all down. A few drops of colostrum? I don't think so.

Luckily Xena didn't appear to know any better, even though she couldn't be bothered making an effort to fill her own belly. Despite the midwives' best efforts to connect lips to nipple, she preferred her manually extracted goo delivered by sterile eye dropper several times a day and night before dozing off contentedly for at least three hours at a time. Her reluctance to do anything involving her mouth and my breasts didn't faze the midwives at this early stage, so we kept the dropper thing happening. For a day or so I was under the impression—soon to be proven wrong—that caring for a baby was a cinch. Squeeze, drip, sleep. A little boring, but not too taxing in the greater scheme of things.

Baby's first feed

During the last few months of pregnancy, your breasts were quietly getting ready for bub's arrival by producing colostrum. You may even have seen a little of this clear-coloured goo leak out of your breasts late in your pregnancy, perhaps immediately after stepping out of a warm shower. This is the pre-milk your baby will drink before your breasts fill up with milk a few days later. Colostrum is filled with antibodies and nourishment for your baby, but is only produced and consumed in tiny amounts. Some babies latch onto their mum's breast immediately after birth and are able to help themselves to wee amounts of the stuff. Others, like my daughter, don't get the hang of feeding from the breast so quickly and prefer to be waited on—remember, they too are recovering from the birth and may not be especially interested in feeding for the first couple of days. If your baby does not drink of his or her own accord, the midwives will show you how to manually extract a few drops of colostrum to be fed to your bub via a teaspoon or a dropper. When your breastmilk arrives, feeding may become an entirely different experience altogether.

Day 2: baby bonding

During a quiet moment together when she wasn't feeding, sleeping or filling her nappy, I nuzzled Xena's head. The Big Guy was at work and the midwives must have been busy with other women's bosoms, having just milked mine for Xena's last feed. 'So little one, when do we bond?' I whispered in her ear. I was a little confused about how and when bonding with Xena would happen. Or had it happened already and I'd missed it?

Most of the information I had read during pregnancy assured me that breast-feeding immediately after the birth created an ideal bonding environment for mother and child. Um, strike one: Xena wasn't the least bit interested in my breasts after the birth. The first few days of breastfeeding further cemented this bond, the books continued authoritatively. Er, strike two: Xena had maintained her boycott of my breasts well into Day Two, which meant she was still being fed hand-expressed colostrum via an eyedropper. If the books were right, Xena looked more likely to form a lasting relationship with a bottle

The birth of mother love

'Bonding' is the word of the moment in parenting, although it's a tricky thing to describe. Basically, it refers to the intense feelings of attachment that develop between you and your baby. Some women swear they felt this the moment they laid eyes on their baby and have had it ever since. Others don't initially feel quite so connected to their baby, and take a little more time to adjust to and love the new person in their life. They discover that attachment to their baby and fiercely maternal feelings grow as the weeks and months go by.

of baby Panadol than she was with her birth mother, all of which wouldn't have surprised me, given my conflicting feelings.

Forty-eight hours after the birth, I was definitely besotted with this living, breathing child, yet she didn't feel like my own. She looked nothing like me, and nothing like how I had imagined. The only visible link between us was the streaks of my dried blood on the top of her head, but their days were numbered as her first bath loomed.

My feelings were strange, confused and contrary to what I had expected. I was overwhelmed by the thought that the infant in my arms was mine. When I held her, I couldn't get close enough, wanting to squeeze her to myself and gobble up her soft fuzzy head. Yet at other times, when she lay sleeping or gazed up at me blankly, I felt like a stranger, watching somebody who looked just like me caring for a baby who, although vaguely familiar, I couldn't quite place. Deep down I knew that woman was me. And I knew that Xena was my child. The relationship just didn't feel set in stone yet.

There's no right way to bond, and there's no correct time frame for this to happen either. As long as you continue to take care of your baby's needs, your relationship and feelings will naturally develop and you will eventually bond even if you don't feel much of a connection at first. In the meantime you can help the process along by:

- having skin-to-skin contact with your baby
- gazing into your baby's eyes during feeding
- massaging your baby gently after a bath
- taking time to marvel at the human being you have made.

Learning the ropes

Life became trickier after Day Two when the live-in help started to withdraw ever so gradually. First the midwives stopped the hand-milking service for the dropper feeds and instructed me to milk myself—something I was not altogether comfortable doing. I could squeeze out the goods; no probs. Catching the stuff was the difficult part. Each drop usually rolled down the nipple and along the underside of my breast, trickling down the outside of the container as opposed to the inside where it needed to go. A week ago, as a journalist, I was chasing stories and meeting deadlines. Now I was chasing drops around my slippery chest and meeting my match in a stupid jar. Go figure.

Putting your new job into perspective

It's probably taken you years to learn the ropes of your profession, master blow-drying the tricky side of your hair or teach yourself guitar. Maybe you're still refining these skills. Your mothering skills will evolve over time, too. So go easy on yourself when each new stage of motherhood baffles you, and submit to the thrill of being thrown in the deep end.

Next the midwives withdrew their nappy-changing support, leaving Xena and me to our own devices with the ridiculous cloth nappies the hospital provided. Unsure of hospital protocol, I had banished all tempting thoughts of asking the Big Guy to smuggle in a packet of Huggies, even though the idea made more sense than wrapping my baby's lower half from navel to knee in non-absorbent material that required an engineering degree to assemble and fasten. The nappy pin was the biggest worry, despite the midwives' assurance that running the pointy end through my hair helped the pin slide smoothly through the two-inch-thick layer of fabric. Now there's a great idea — encourage a woman who's just endured the biggest physical ordeal of her life to point a sharp object at her head before ramming it towards her baby's belly.

Like the cloth nappy situation, I was a little disappointed in the bottom-cleaning equipment the hospital provided. Cotton balls and a surgical dish of water were a tad too basic for my liking. Oh yes, and BYO elbow grease. Having forgotten the midwives' grim warning to assemble everything I needed for a nappy change before actually undoing the dirty nappy, disappointment quickly turned into disbelief upon discovering that Xena had kicked up a storm in the contents of her nappy, which I had left undone while I, er, went to fetch my nappy-change supplies. I thought wistfully about the unopened packet of fragrant baby wipes sitting neatly on the change table at home, just waiting to commence employment.

After a fairly futile attempt to wipe away some of the mess, I gave up and buzzed for reinforcement. 'There's some serious shit going down here', I tried to joke with the midwife on duty, but she was clearly unimpressed, herding us off to the nursery to master my next challenge: learning how to bath my revolting baby. The message was pretty clear. You made a mistake, you clean it up. I may have been residing in a hospital full of babycare experts, but they were here for back-up — not room service.

Poo to you, too!

Welcome to the grossly absorbing world of baby poo. And what an ever-changing world it is.

Your baby's first poo will shock the living daylights out of you. It will appear sometime during the first few days after the birth as a great big wad of sticky, green-black stuff that seems impossible to remove from bub's bum without a high-pressure hose. This first poo is called meconium, and it's a mixture of bile, mucous and other secretions that have built up in your baby's intestines. The good news is that meconium represents a passing phase of poo. Once that's all out of bub's system, the real poo settles in.

Breastfed babies' poo is fairly innocuous. It tends to be yellow-brown, unformed (think: a big splat of mustard) and not especially offensive to the nose. Bottle-fed babies pass poos that are darker, more formed and, sadly, smellier. Yet another good reason to try to breastfeed for as long as you can!

When your baby starts solid food, more fun is in store as you wonder at all the little bits and bobs that start appearing in the poop. For the common but harmless culprits that tend to freak out first-time parents, see 'What goes in must come out' on page 159.

Chapter 3

Maternity ward *mayhem*

Day 3

I woke up with a start, jolted into consciousness by the most inconsiderate of my neighbours. This was the one who watched crappy movies at night while the rest of us tried unsuccessfully to block out her guffaws with strategically placed pillows.

'*Where* did he stab ya?' she barked into the phone. 'Well sucked in Dazza, you shoulda been here with me!' Oh how I hated sharing a room. I lay still for a few moments trying to imagine life with a partner who engaged in stabbing brawls while his baby's head engaged in the birth canal when I felt a sharp pain in my upper chest. Either I had an extremely vivid imagination, or someone had replaced my uncomfortable hospital bed with an even more uncomfortable bed of rocks.

And then I realised that the stabbing pain was caused by the contents of my pyjama top.

Rolling over onto my back, I almost cried out in shock from the weight of my front. My chest was hot, hard, heavy and hurt like hell. I no longer had two soft and pliable bosoms, each able to take their rightful place in a single bra cup. That morning I resembled a walking cliff. There was no sign of cleavage, just an enormous drop. So this is what the midwives mean by that strange expression 'milk comes in'. Well I didn't like it. Somebody take the damn milk away.

The Big Guy reacted with typical male candour when he rocked up a few hours later. 'Whoa, Mumma!' he enthused appreciatively. 'Check 'em out!' With a new daughter and an impressively stacked wife, it was fairly obvious that the Big Guy was feeling pretty pleased with life.

I, however, was not so impressed with this latest shock to my already shocked-off-my-rocks existence, especially when word got round

When your milk comes in

This sudden influx of milk into your breasts is known as 'engorgement' and, for many women, it is not a comfortable time—although it is reassuring to know your body is actually producing milk. It takes a few weeks before your body works out the supply and demand system needed for your particular mum-and-bub combination. When this eventually happens, your breasts will still fill up with milk before every feed, but not to the extent that they feel as though they will explode. So hang in there—it won't feel this way forever!

In the meantime, you can relieve the symptoms of engorgement by:

- wearing a supportive maternity bra—day and night

that the milk bar was now open for business. The midwives suddenly went into a frenzy trying to encourage Xena to drink from my monstrous protrusions. 'Now, let's see some action', they chortled delightedly as Xena woke crying. The assumption seemed to be that breastmilk was the missing piece in the mother–baby relationship puzzle. I had learnt to bath my baby and change my baby and, once my milk came in, I would also be able to feed my baby. Everything would be okay from then on in.

Hmmm, I wasn't so sure. The arrival of my milk certainly didn't come with a side order of confidence in myself as a parent; it simply meant I had an extra task to master, and a little voice in the back of my head whispering that if the dropper scenario was any indication, the job wouldn't be as easy as I'd previously imagined.

More than ever I felt like a complete fraud. And as the day dragged on, I also began to feel remarkably bovine. Gentle pressure on me now produced a steady squirt

- feeding your baby frequently. If the nipple is too firm for your baby to latch on to properly, express enough milk so that your nipple area becomes soft again

- gently massaging full or lumpy breasts using a downward motion while your baby is feeding

- applying cold packs after feeding

- putting rinsed and dried fresh green cabbage leaves inside your bra, with a hole cut out in the middle for each nipple

- asking your carer which pain relief is suitable for you if you are in pain.

If at any time during feeding you are in pain, see blood in your milk or on your breast or feel a bit fluey, seek medical advice. Pain during feeding is often due to feeding technique, but can also be a sign of infection developing. If in any doubt, check it out.

of milk. All I needed was a metal pail and a milkmaid; I grimaced, while great handfuls of my breast were thrust into poor Xena's unsuspecting— and obviously unwilling—mouth. As streams of milk sprayed across her scrunched-up face it was obvious that Xena still didn't want a bar of this, despite the relentless pressure. Might have had something to do with the bedside brigade positioning her for these first feeds in such a way that she looked like a snake ready to fang into its prey. Perhaps she also resented having her head repeatedly butted against my rock-hard chest. I know I certainly did.

Undercover cover

Pop a waterproof cot mattress protector under the fitted sheet on your side of the bed once you get home to help absorb the inevitable night-time overflow that tends to drench your nightie, sheets and even your partner!

The prognosis

After the first half-hour of repeated Xena-to-chest butting attempts, a fair amount of squeezing out excess milk and a different opinion from each midwife who assisted with the so-called feed, I was emotionally drained. The torpedoes on my chest, however, remained bra-bustingly full and Xena let us know in no uncertain terms that she was over the whole exercise. I was quickly milked to provide an expressed feed for my hot, bothered and hungry baby. We made repeated attempts throughout the day before Xena was declared tongue-tied ('that's why she can't suck properly'), not tongue-tied ('look, she sucks my finger!') and possibly suffering from jaundice ('she's looking a bit yellow, which could mean she's jaundiced, tired and can't be bothered to suck'). And finally, the clanger: I had flat nipples. To that I felt like saying, 'come and see me on a cold day'.

To my mortification, the flat nipples diagnosis appeared to be the winner and I was presented with a silicone shield, which was supposed to draw up my flesh to form a pseudo-perky number that Xena just wouldn't be able to resist. As I settled back for another round of manhandling and head-to-breast butting, I couldn't help noticing the ironic difference between my expectations of that moment and the reality. I had walked into motherhood with nothing less than a Hallmark approach.

Birth, baby and breastfeeding

In an ideal world, you'd give birth without complications and place your baby immediately against your bare breast, which bub would latch onto with ease and suckle away happily. But it doesn't always happen this way, especially if you and your baby had a tough time at birth.

It's widely accepted that certain pain-relieving drugs, such as pethidine, pass through the placenta to your baby and can stay in your baby's system for a few days after the delivery. This can make your newborn feel a bit drowsy and affect his or her ability to feed. A forceps delivery or vacuum extraction (ventouse) may also affect your first breastfeeding attempts, as your baby may be a bit sore and cranky after being forcibly evicted from his or her previous safe haven in the womb. Other factors that may impede first feeding attempts include a high palette or tongue-tie in your baby—do make sure you get professional advice to confirm this diagnosis though, and don't take a suggestion as gospel.

Finally, consider how your carers are 'helping' you to establish feeding. Would you like someone to ram your head into your dinner plate to teach you to eat? Hmm, thought not. Your baby might also resist a forceful introduction to your breast, so go gently and don't let anyone push either of you around.

I pictured myself cradling my newborn baby in my arms, gazing down lovingly as my child's lips snuffled sweetly towards my breast and contentedly drank her fill before drifting calmly and quietly off to sleep. Quite possibly piped music played in the background while a handsome half-naked male servant served peeled grapes and fanned us down with the branch of a tropical palm tree—no relation to Hallmark there, but still, a girl can dream. After spending only a few hours trying to live up to my own warm-and-fuzzy expectations, I felt like rejecting the role of nurturing earth mother and embracing a tin of formula and a nice big bottle. Preferably a cold bottle of bubbly resting in an ice bucket between the Big Guy and me as we dined at our favourite restaurant. Strangely enough, I couldn't quite fit Xena into that picture.

🐛🐛🐛

The day limped along, and by nightfall I was an emotional wreck. The final straw was when one of the friendlier

Establishing breastfeeding

If you're seriously struggling to master the art of breastfeeding in the early days, being told it can take six weeks before it becomes second nature can sound like a very good reason to quit trying. Try to remember that not every single feed during this time is going to be as hard or as frustrating as your early attempts. You may have some successes as well as what seem like failures, but it should gradually improve bit by bit. In the meantime, try the following things to help you get through the worst times:

• Pat yourself on the back when a feed goes well, and shrug off the ones you'd rather forget. Experienced breastfeeders will tell you midwives confided that successful breastfeeding could take up to six weeks to establish. Gulp. Six weeks? She had to be joking. I had things to do, including getting a life back, and I couldn't possibly do those things if I was bound to a flat-nipple-rejecting baby for the better part of two months. It was all too much to contemplate, so I did the next best thing: crumpled in a heap and sobbed my little heart out. The kindly midwife reassured me that most mums felt teary when their milk came in, largely as a result of the tidal wave of hormones that flooded in at the same time. She also insisted that, even though life felt very strange and overwhelming at that moment, I would soon become a confident mother and things like feeding and caring for Xena would come naturally. I bet she said that to all the new mums. I wondered if anyone seriously believed her.

After a shocking night of watching helplessly as Xena dodged my chest and gagged on wayward sprays of breastmilk, I decided the only thing that really sucked was the process

the key to overcoming a rocky start is to take it one day—or even one feed —at a time.

- Experiment with different breastfeeding positions and ways of attaching your baby to find what works for you.

- Keep an open mind when listening to all the advice you receive in hospital, and ask to speak to a lactation consultant if you become confused by conflicting advice measured out by different midwives on different shifts.

- Join the Australian Breastfeeding Association. You can find it online at <www.breastfeeding. asn.au> or via its national breastfeeding helpline: 1800 mum 2 mum (1800 686 2 686).

of breastfeeding. Nevertheless, I soldiered on, believing that breastfeeding, with or without an artificial attachment, was The Right Thing to do. All the literature I had diligently read backed up that belief, pitting breastmilk's impressive number of health benefits against the paltry 'convenience' or the 'you're so slack but at least your partner can help care for your poor baby if she takes a bottle' pros of infant formula. Never once did it occur to me to question whether there were exceptions to every rule, or to consider that quite possibly I could be one of them. If breastfeeding was good enough for the World Health Organisation to recommend to the entire female population, then it was good enough for me. I had no experience in this game so I would do what I was told. At the very least I would bust my bosoms trying.

More than anything, I longed to feed my baby *au naturel*, just like the other three women in our shared room, but Xena continued her hunger strike even though the midwives insisted we would break her down by sheer persistence. The other women didn't seem to have as many problems as Xena and I had. In fact, many of them almost made breastfeeding look graceful, bringing their petite babies to their petite breasts following minimal instruction other than perhaps the odd tweak from an approving midwife standing watch. I was insanely jealous of one mum in particular. Even if her three other young children hadn't come to visit, I could tell she'd graduated from a far more advanced school of feeding than the rest of us had. When her baby boy woke crying for his next feed, she'd calmly and confidently pick him up, lob out a breast—which he always took without so much as a whimper—and sit sedately in the armchair by her bed while he filled his belly. After a gentle backrub, which never failed to produce a discreet release of air, she would then wrap him up and put him straight back down in his cot, where he'd sleep soundly until he needed more sustenance. Watching that woman curl up in bed to read or sleep between feeds, I desperately wanted to be her—minus the three extra kids. Going through this once was hard enough, but three more times would tip me over the edge. Then and there I vowed to stop at one child: Xena would just have to put up with being an only child.

Friends with babies would visit during the day, enquiring politely, 'How's feeding going?' I was tempted to answer that feeding was 'going' to drive me crazy unless a miracle happened, but, knowing that they were all feeding or had fed their babies breastmilk for the first six months, I just said we were working on it and quickly changed the subject. Nobody asked me if I was having problems and, for some stupid reason, I didn't tell anyone. Was there a code of silence imposed on all women who had disastrous experiences with breastfeeding or who didn't breastfeed at all? Did any of these women actually exist, besides my mother? Good old sensible Mum couldn't see what all the fuss was about. Watching Xena and I flounder around during a feed and seeing my frustration and tension levels soaring, Mum politely asked to make a suggestion. 'Go ahead,' I dared, 'tell me something

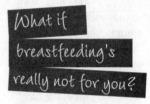

What if breastfeeding's really not for you?

A happy, healthy mum who enjoys looking after her baby is of much more value to your family than breastfeeding if it's clearly not working or making both you and your baby miserable. If you really can't or don't want to breastfeed, don't. Last time I looked, there were two ways to feed a baby.

about breastfeeding that I haven't heard in the last 24 hours'. 'If it's not working, put her on the bottle', she said simply. 'I fed all four of you with formula from the day you were born and there's nothing wrong with any of you.'

Those were pretty much the exact words I wanted to hear, but I didn't want to hear them from Mum. She'd had her babies decades ago, when formula hadn't had the evil reputation of usurper of the breast that it had today. I wanted the current experts—the studies, the research and the midwives—to say that not breastfeeding was okay; after all, they were the ones who had scared the life out of me with their ominous predictions of eczema, asthma, obesity, low immunity and generally reprehensible health in formula-fed babies. Until those people gave me the green light, I would persevere with the challenge. So I thanked Mum very much for the advice and asked her to pass me a fresh nipple shield on her way out.

Bottle basics

Bottle-feeding advice from early childhood experts is notoriously hard to come by, as you won't find many who are willing to advocate formula over breastmilk for newborns. Your best bet is to find a good GP who can shed some unbiased light on the subject.

Plans B, C, D and E

With every shift change at the hospital came a new approach to our mission, as the midwife on duty promptly dismissed everything the previous one had told me. Reigning in my usually assertive opinions, I submitted docilely to each new suggestion or technique. Basically, I gave everything a shot. Interestingly enough, the only apparent consensus among my carers was that the nipple shield was only ever to be used as a last resort. The midwives appeared to hate the stupid thing as much as I did, which made me wonder why I was even using it, until a new midwife charged into the room on a mission to banish the shield for good.

'Don't even think about using this thing', she blustered in disgust, plucking the offending piece of silicone from the container of sterilising fluid it called home when not in use. 'Don't you know it will reduce your milk supply?' After a cursory inspection of my chest, she charged off to retrieve a clean cloth nappy, which she rolled up and wedged firmly under lefty, the obvious choice for the next feed since it was already dripping with engorgement. A few deft hand movements got rid of the overspill and returned it to partial softness, and then the midwife laid Xena across the pillow on my lap. She brought Xena up into position, while simultaneously cupping my skin with her forefinger and thumb to secure a big wedge. Stop the press! Xena actually latched on—and what's more, she was sucking! 'Your breasts are just too big', the midwife informed me. 'The towel brings the nipple up to a better level for her mouth.' Well there you go. Those big boobs had done it again. They were embarrassing in primary school when I yearned to be as flat as my friends. They played havoc with my teenage mind in high school, when they attracted more attention than the rest of me. And now they made breastfeeding harder than it should have been. If nothing else, at least they were consistently difficult to live with.

Money talks

Much has been said about the health benefits of breastfeeding, and now here's the clincher: breastfeeding is sooo much cheaper than buying formula, bottles, teats and cleaning equipment for the next 12 months. Work out what you'll save—then go and spend it on a holiday with your partner and your baby (or perhaps several pairs of fabulous shoes!).

Xena continued to suck away, dragging the end of my breast into a semi-flat spout. I wasn't entirely comfortable, but she was finally drinking straight from the source so I didn't dare move in case I disturbed her rhythm. Poised awkwardly and waiting for her to finish, I became conscious of a growing sense of achievement.

Wouldn't you know it, the thrill was short-lived. Not only did that first non-shield feed only last for five minutes before Xena fell away and refused to latch back on again, but after two more attempts her interest in feeding waned completely.

The surprising truth about breastfeeding

Lots of women find breast-feeding easy and natural, but judging by the national breastfeeding statistics, many more find it one of the trickiest aspects of motherhood to master. It appears that, while 80 per cent of Australian women try breastfeeding, less than 20 per cent are still breastfeeding by the time their babies reach six months. This is a far cry from the National Health and Medical Research Council's recommendation that mums should breastfeed their babies exclusively for the first six months and then continue, in conjunction with solid food, until the age of 12 months. The NHMRC's guidelines reflect the World Health Organisation's breastfeeding policy, which goes one step further and advocates mothers breastfeed their infants up until the age of two.

While it's important to bear in mind that the WHO's advice is designed to cover the situation of every mum in every country around the world (including countries where mothers don't have access to clean water and formula, and entire populations that are plagued with illness and infection), it's definitely worth at least trying to breastfeed your baby.

The first real hiccup

At the same time as our struggle to make breastfeeding work, the daily blood test to monitor Xena's ever-yellowing skin concluded that the slight jaundice she had presented with at birth had developed to such an extent that she needed treatment. Unless the jaundice was halted by a stint under UV light, Xena's energy and interest in feeding would continue to decrease. Her treatment felt like a jail sentence: 36 hours in the phototherapy unit in the nursery, only to be taken out for the time it took to administer three-hourly feeds of breastmilk.

It all happened so fast that I didn't quite know what to make of it, except that I was seriously scared. Xena had been pronounced healthy and alert at birth, and now she needed help to overcome a condition I didn't really understand. The Big Guy was with us when we took Xena to the phototherapy unit. Realising my baby girl was to spend a day and a half on her own in that box, lying under the long blue light bulbs, I began sobbing uncontrollably. Clutching onto the Big Guy for dear life, I cried all the way back to my room, which seemed pathetically empty without Xena in it. In between great gasping sobs I tried to articulate to the Big Guy my biggest fears: would my girl know me after our forced separation? Would she think I had abandoned her? Would she forget I was her mum?

The birth of the blues

On day three or four, when your chest is feeling waterlogged, you'll most likely turn on the waterworks, too. You may feel teary, a bit flat or sad, and unable to cope with minor things. This is known as the baby blues, and is widely thought to be a result of massive hormonal changes. Run with it, the tide will go out again soon.

Phototherapy

Those three hours between dropping Xena off at the phototherapy unit (or 'the Box', as we called it) and our first scheduled feed were interminably long. Suddenly, my whole attitude had changed. I had been so focused on learning to breastfeed that, in my mind, Xena had simply become one of the elements of that baffling process. We had struggled through each feed and then I'd put her back down in her cot, glad to reclaim my body and some personal space, and not-so-glad to see that my own meal had usually been delivered and gone lukewarm in the meantime. Now that Xena had been taken from my side, I missed her terribly and wanted her back. A strange case of absence makes the heart grow fonder perhaps, even though she was only two minutes down the hall.

The Big Guy wouldn't leave my side until he knew that both Xena and I were okay, which was just as well because I needed a shoulder to cry on for a good 20 minutes or so before I could steel myself to go and see our daughter in captivity. Tears threatened to spill again as I saw the box but

Golden child

Many newborn babies start to look a little yellow, or unusually tanned, by day two or three. It first becomes noticeable in the face, after which the colour floods down to the rest of the body, and even tints the whites of the eyes slightly yellow. Jaundice also makes babies feel very sleepy, and consequently uninterested in feeding.

Newborn jaundice occurs when a baby's immature liver is unable to process the excess bilirubin in his or her blood.

gave way to a chuckle when we saw Xena. The midwives had stripped her bare and she lay naked, but for a Fearless Fly–like mask to protect her eyes from the rays. She lay on her tummy, knees tucked up under her chest and with her beautifully round bottom tilted cheekily upwards. Her face was turned towards us, and her sweet little mouth was slightly open as she slept peacefully under the rays. We nudged each other, delighted to see her looking so comfortable and so content. At four days old she was all class.

By then I was composed enough to actually ask some questions without breaking down again, so the

From partners to parents

One minute you're a loved-up couple, dreaming of the day you'll hold your baby in your arms. The next minute you've got a newborn baby hogging all your attention, kisses and cuddles! Make a pact with your partner to wrap your arms around each other at least once a day so you guys stay close, too.

midwives filled us in. The plan was to wake Xena every three hours for a feed. The combination of UV rays and frequent feeds would combat the excessive bilirubin levels in her blood that resulted in jaundice. We also discovered that the

Bilirubin is basically old blood that your body used to process for your baby while bub was still hanging around in your womb. It's more common in babies who were born premature, with an infection, or who have a different blood group to their mother. Jaundice can also present in babies who are born with a lot of bruising, as a result of ventouse or forceps extraction. Mild jaundice often fades away on its own accord. Otherwise, the usual treatment is a stint in a phototherapy box, where your baby lies naked, but with eye protection, under UV lights that help break down the bilirubin and restore normal skin tone.

jaundice was quite possibly caused by her vacuum extraction into the world, so at least it all started to make sense. Most importantly, we were assured that Xena wasn't in any danger. Once the treatment was completed she would be fine.

Convinced that Xena was as safe and happy as a newborn could be, we left her to catch some rays and went for a walk outside to do the same. Sunshine, fresh air and an ice-cream from the hospital kiosk proved marvellous therapy, as did spending some one-on-one time with the Big Guy. For the first time in what felt like a long time, but had only been a few days, we enjoyed a physical closeness. The weight of his arm across my shoulder gave me the comfort and strength I needed to walk back into the hospital and face the next challenge. My other option—the one I kept to myself—had been to smuggle myself out of this place in his car.

I arrived back in the nursery to find the midwives holding Xena, who was dressed in a fresh nappy and singlet. Glancing at the clock, I saw it was still another 30 minutes until our next feed. I was told she had just—how would one put this delicately?—redecorated the entire back wall of the phototherapy box. I shouldn't have laughed, but I did. That cheeky upturned bottom had fired a salvo at the merciless kidnappers who had locked her in a box, away from her mum. I was becoming more fond of my girl by the minute.

We decided it was as good a time as any for a feed, so I offered Xena my full side—again and again and again. Unsurprisingly, Xena wasn't interested in attaching, let alone sucking, so the midwives quickly expressed the milk instead. Another nipple shield—I thought I had finished with these things!—was placed over my breast. The open end of a long thin supply line was placed under the shield, near the holes, while the other end attached to an enormous syringe that was filled with my milk. As Xena was brought to the shield, the midwife holding the syringe gently depressed the plunger, which sent a light stream of milk coursing through the line, out of the shield and into her mouth. Xena hardly had to move a muscle. And I'd thought our previous feeds were a major production! 'Why don't we just give her the milk in a bottle?' I asked, thinking this would be far less labour-intensive. 'Oh no, dear', the midwives explained. Apparently, this fake feeding rigmarole would reinforce to Xena that breasts and babies must work together to fill tummies. Fast-food joints such as bottles were to be discouraged, if not completely ignored. Come heaven or high water, we would make that girl feed from the natural source.

Express yourself

You may have heard some breastfeeding mums make analogies between themselves and cows. They are referring to the process of manually extracting their breastmilk, which is also known as 'expressing'. There are many reasons why you might want to express your breastmilk: your baby may be sick or premature and therefore not strong enough to suck; or perhaps your baby hasn't quite figured out how to extract breastmilk directly from its natural source. You may also want to express and store excess milk if your breasts are too full and uncomfortable. You can express milk by your own hand (although you'll have a frightful time trying to get the stuff into a container with this method), or via a hand-held or electric pump, both of which can channel the milk directly into a bottle or storage bag. Some mums swear by the hand-helds, others say they couldn't have survived without an electric pump. The latter, incidentally, will make you feel most bovine of all, as they really do operate like the milking machines on dairy farms! Electric pumps are also very expensive, so either hire one or wait until you're really sure you'll be pumping longterm before splashing out on the bee's knees of equipment.

Funnily enough I ended up enjoying those feeds, as they actually became quite easy—much more so than our previous breastfeeding attempts back out in the ward.

Fifteen minutes before each feed I expressed as much as I could from one side and then brought it into the nursery. I would then wake sleepy Xena by lifting her out of her box and dressing her in a clean nappy and singlet. Then we would perform our shield/supply line/ syringe number before I undressed my girl and put her back down to sleep. The rigid schedule gave me a sense of purpose and responsibility that I hadn't felt before and much of my stress vanished as the supply line feeding worked so efficiently. I could simply enjoy cradling my girl as she lay in my arms and swallowed the milk. I began to see Xena as an entity on her own, not just an attachment to my breast that didn't work so well.

Takeaway meals for bub

Expressing excess milk in the early days, when you are squirtingly full, has great benefits. You can stockpile these feeds in storage bags or containers in the freezer for up to three months, making it possible for someone else to thaw them out and give bub a breastmilk feed when you can't.

The entire exercise was over in about 20 minutes—that included expressing the milk—which meant I had well over two hours to myself in between feeds. For the first time in four days, I made some phone calls, watched a little TV and catnapped. The phone calls in particular did me the world of good. I spoke to some friends and colleagues back out in the real world who were gratifyingly effusive in their congratulations. Feeling more relaxed than I had all week, I could finally share some of their excitement.

Xena's 36-hour phototherapy sentence passed very quickly, her condition improving all the time. By the time she was returned to her cot by my bedside, she had lost her soft yellow glow. I, on the other hand, had gained a warm and fuzzy glow, because by then I had fallen head over heels in love with that beautiful child.

Why some midwives are pro-expressing but anti-bottles

Why not just give a baby who won't breastfeed a bottle of expressed breastmilk? Well, the theory is that your baby may become accustomed to extracting milk from the bottle teat, which is physically easier than extracting milk from the breast, and that this will adversely affect subsequent breastfeeding attempts. For this reason you may be advised against offering your baby a bottle until you and your baby have got the breastfeeding thing down pat, which is generally thought to be by around six weeks.

That's not to say all babies will have trouble switching from breast to the occasional bottle, though. I've certainly heard of many mums who have used bottles in the short term to keep the breastmilk intake going until they mastered the art of breastfeeding. And it's important to note that many of the bottles and teats on the market have been designed in conjunction with all sorts of lactation experts in a bid to make bottle-feeding as much like breastfeeding as possible. If a bottle helps you feed your baby breastmilk for longer than would otherwise be possible, how on earth could that be a bad thing?

Chapter 4

Newborn
know-how

On day six we were finally given the all clear to go home. In less than a week I had been changed forever. My body had changed, my mind had changed and my life had changed. Most significantly, my relationship with my bed had changed. A full night's sleep at the end of a full day was no longer a given. At most, I could duck off to bed for quick but sporadic comfort visits, after which I was turfed out to get on with the business of being Xena's mum. Still unsure of what to make of this new life, one thing was clear: the Big Guy and I were no longer on our own. A third little person had wriggled her way into our hearts and, despite our underlying fear that we had absolutely no idea what to do with her, we felt very lucky to have her.

In hospital the thought of going home had been both exciting and scary. I was excited because I couldn't wait to get on with life as a family. But I was scared, too, mainly about the nights. What would happen if I couldn't settle Xena? Who would I buzz when I needed confirmation that she had latched on properly, was sucking well and getting enough milk? Would I ever sleep for longer than two hours again? Even though the midwives had pretty much left us alone for our last day and night in hospital, just knowing they were there had been comforting. Suddenly I regretted not signing up for the parentcraft classes that I had knocked back on the premise that 'she's a baby—how hard could it be?'

Expert advice on tap

Do some research before you need it and identify a few lifelines for those 'What to do now?' moments. Invaluable resources that you can access from home include the following:

- *general babycare helplines.* To find the parenting helpline in your state or territory, visit <www.raisingchildren.net. au/articles/hotlines> then stash the number in your mobile phone and don't be afraid to call when you need to—even if it's 2 am.

- *breastfeeding support.* The Australian Breastfeeding Association has a phone line and a website where you can find information and submit questions. It also runs breastfeeding courses. You'll find it at <www. breastfeeding.asn.au> or on the national freecall number 1800 mum 2 mum (1800 686 2 686).

- *health advice for you and your family.* Healthdirect is a 24-hour telephone line staffed by registered nurses to provide over-the-phone advice for you and your family for free (unless you call from your mobile).

Walking through the front door of our home was disconcerting. This had nothing to do with the horrendous state of the kitchen—which looked like an abandoned scientific experiment—and everything to do with the realisation that I was now totally responsible for Xena. What should I do with her? I stood around feeling awkward for a moment, watching Xena unconsciously blow tiny spit bubbles as she lay cradled in my arms. I'd already fed and changed her before we left hospital, so that ruled out both of those possibilities as things to do with her. And she was awake in my arms, so I figured sleep wasn't on the cards—worse luck, as I could have done with a kip myself. Having literally no idea what to do with my daughter, I took her on a grand tour of the house.

It's currently available to residents in all states and territories except Queensland and Victoria, although it's scheduled to be a fully national service by 2011. Call 1800 02 222.

- *your maternity hospital.* In the first few days after going home, you should be able to call and ask advice from the midwives in the hospital you gave birth in.

- *general practitioner.* If you don't already have a trusty GP, now's the time to find one and sign up as a patient. Don't wait until you have a sick baby on your hands. On that note, it's also worth making friends with your local pharmacist, who can be a great first port of call for minor ailments such as teething or nappy rash.

- *local resources.* Your maternity hospital and early childhood health centre can also point you in the direction of local experts (such as lactation consultants) and early parenting classes. Use them! At the very least, visiting your childhood health centre gets you out of the house and into the company of other like-minded people. At best, you might actually learn something useful!

The Big Guy had done his best to clean up for what looked like about two minutes before he had picked us up. By the look of his eyes and the smell of his breath he'd spent more time wetting the baby's head than wetting the dishcloth. And who could blame him? I'd have done the same myself had the midwives given me half a chance. Trouble was that every time I wheeled Xena around to the nursery for a few moments of peace, some zealous do-gooder ended up wheeling her straight back in to me, espousing the benefits of rooming with my new little attachment. There had been no sign of the complimentary night of babysitting other mums assured me was presented to them during their hospital stay. Yet another myth of motherhood?

Why silence isn't always golden

When you don't have other children, a house can be very quiet—and that's not always a good thing when you want your baby to sleep well during the day.

It means phones, loud trucks thundering down your street or a dropped saucepan will easily jolt your baby awake before he or she's had enough sleep to wake up happy and refreshed.

And a still-tired baby can be frustratingly difficult to care for. Try to create a background hum of music, television or radio during the day to disguise the sudden loud noises that are part and parcel of domestic life and help lull your baby to sleep.

Mums of two, three or more babies will attest to the fact that their younger ones learnt very quickly to sleep through absolutely anything, including shrieking siblings fighting over the noisiest of electronic toys and futile cries of 'Shhh! Don't wake the baby!'.

By the time I was through inspecting the damage caused by the Big Guy's brief return to bachelorhood, Xena was sound asleep and oblivious to the nervous tension she had unwittingly created. All of a sudden I was struck by the enormity of those first moments in our own space as a family. Choking back the tears, I told the Big Guy that I was taking my girl to bed, and would he like to join us? He readily agreed, muttering encouraging words about bonding when I knew that what he really meant was 'bewdy, now I can get some sleep!' So we choofed off to the boudoir to enjoy a mid-morning siesta.

Xena, however, had other ideas, choosing to open her eyes and test out her lungs the moment her head touched our mattress. Unperturbed, I decided her crying was rather cute, certainly not irritating in the least, and reasoned that Xena was probably more used to sleeping on her own, given that she did so fabulously in hospital. Her beautiful new bassinette, complete with expensive designer baby sheets and mosquito net, was much cosier than the plastic box in which she slept in hospital.

Tiny tummies

It helps to know that your baby isn't demanding to be fed at all hours (including ungodly ones!) just for the fun of disrupting your sleep. A newborn's stomach is said to be the size of a marble at birth, and this is why it needs regular refilling. Amazing, huh?

She stopped crying when I picked her up and carried her into her room. Yep, good move. But uh oh, she'd started again the moment I began to lower her into the bassinette, gaining volume and intensity when I lay her down completely. Okay, now her crying was a little more irritating than before and confusing, since she hadn't behaved like that in hospital. There, she'd fed slept, fed and slept some more. Surely she didn't need another feed? Her last one had been just over an hour ago.

Crying checklist

All babies cry and in the early days you too can be reduced to tears, trying to work out what on earth is upsetting bub. Until you feel more confident working out what your baby's trying to tell you, ask yourself if he or she could be:

- hungry
- tired or overtired
- uncomfortable in a soiled or wet nappy
- hot or cold
- unwell or in pain.

If you have ruled out all these options and bub still won't sleep, the easiest option is to surrender to the idea that you'll need to somehow lull the baby to sleep. If bub is really wound up, pop him or her in a sling while you go about your chores or the pram and take him or her for a walk—bub will most likely be soothed by the movement and doze off. Or, if it doesn't bother you to simply curl up on the couch with the baby snuggled up in your arms as you watch something mindless on TV, feel free to indulge.

If your baby continues to cry inconsolably or in a high-pitched tone, it's worth getting him or her checked out by your GP to rule out any medical cause.

I shuffled back to our bedroom, nestling Xena to my chest, to confer with the Big Guy. Secretly I was hoping he would leap up from the bed, offer to take over and magically settle her to sleep. From the helpless look he gave me I knew I was waiting in vain. 'Maybe she needs another feed', he offered half-heartedly. 'I wish I could help…' he continued lamely. My heart sank and I tried hard to swallow my disappointment. I was the one with the bosoms, so I was the one tied by the nipple shield to this enigmatic little creature. Pathetically tired, I tried to recall the last time I'd had such little sleep over the period of a week. There was Schoolies' Week on the Gold Coast at the end of high school many years ago, but even then we could catch up on lost sleep at night by sleeping away the days. I didn't want a whole day—I just wanted a few hours and for that luxury I was prepared to pay top dollar.

I tried one more time to put her down to sleep, but I only became more frustrated as my sleeping baby turned into my crying baby the moment her chest left mine. There was no option but to feed her. Again. Her last feed had begun exactly one-and-a-half hours ago. Where were these four-hourly feeds I'd heard rumours about? Where were the two-to-three hour blocks of sleep the baby books urged me to use as my own sleeping time? Where had my life gone?

Keep your tension to yourself

There's no research behind what I'm about to say, but I swear it's true: your baby senses when you are nervous about putting him to bed. As a result, bub won't settle and you'll become even more tense, and so a vicious cycle is created. Be confident about your bedtime technique so your baby picks up on your positive vibes and complies.

🐝 🐝 🐝

Choking back the tears, I tried hard not to resent the Big Guy's luck: his physical inability to produce breastmilk had given him an unfair advantage in this parenting lark. He could sleep whenever he wanted to. I could only sleep whenever Xena let me. 'It's [sob] not [sob] fair [sob]', I blubbered into our bedroom, prodding the Big Guy with my foot, as both my arms were occupied clutching, patting and rubbing my equally distraught baby to my chest. 'I [sob] need [sob] your [sob] help [sob].'

To his credit, the Big Guy promptly rolled himself out of bed to keep me company, even though there really wasn't a thing he could do in the breastfeeding department.

Instead he made himself useful, turning on the TV and busying himself in the kitchen making me tea and opening up a new packet of Tim Tams for my contemplation. He arranged them on a side table near my feeding throne, the hitherto never-used armchair, soon to become strewn with chuck rugs, nipple shields, baby bibs and streaks of milky white stains. 'Waistline be damned', I declared as I chomped down on a biscuit and Xena finally stopped fussing for long enough to chomp down on my shield-encased breast.

Feed you, feed me

Breastfeeding is hungry work. Every time you sit down to feed your baby, have a glass of water or a hydrating drink nearby and something healthy to snack on. A great once-a-day sustaining snack is a smoothie, made with fruit, low-fat milk and a dollop of low-fat yoghurt.

Breastfeeding was still very much a work in progress that hadn't been helped by the 36-hour interlude of supply line feeding. Far from reinforcing to Xena that sucking at the breast resulted in food glorious food, this process had only taught her to open her mouth and receive her milk with minimal effort. So it was back to the silicone shield for us. We'd given bare breast a good shot, but enough was enough. Here was a girl who liked her meals to be served up on a silver platter, but couldn't be bothered cooking. As frustrating as this was, I could see her point — she was shaping up to be a girl after my own heart.

It ended up being a pretty good feed. Ten minutes of sucking turned into a nice snooze, her lips firmly attached to the shield. Wriggling my index finger in the corner of her mouth, I broke her grip and sat her up on my lap, delighted to see for the first time that 'milk drunk' look the midwives had told me about. Her chin rested in my hand as I rubbed her back to help the burp escape. The Big Guy cracked up at his stupefied daughter. Eyes closed and head tilted back, a dribble of milk escaped from the corner of her wide-open mouth. It was obvious the Big Guy was starting to relate to his new daughter.

I carried my sleeping bundle into her room and lay her down in her cot, tensing momentarily as she went to stir and seemed to want to open her eyes, until she settled back down to sleep with a sigh. She wasn't as neatly wrapped in her bunny rug as she had been in hospital, as I still didn't have the knack, but it would have to do.

Pardon you!

The benefits of burping your baby are debatable, according to the experts, but jeez it's satisfying when she produces a whopper! You can help bub burp after each feed by propping him or her into a sitting position, supporting the head so that it's upright and rubbing or patting his or her back, but don't be too worried if bub fails to produce anything of note. It's not dangerous for a baby to go back to bed without belching. If some trapped wind does eventually bother him or her, bub will let you know, and usually the air will escape the moment you pick him or her up.

More than half of all babies will also follow through, with a little spit or up-chuck of milk after a feed. This is called 'posseting' and while it's annoying, messy and potentially ruinous of fabric-covered sofas, it's perfectly normal.

If your baby is a little chucker, the following tips might help minimise the damage:

- Keep a handtowel (aka chuck rug) close by when feeding.

- Keep bub upright for 20 minutes or so after each feed.

- Cover your couch!

- Always check the back of your shirt and the tops of your shoes for milky snail trails before you go out.

The Big Guy and I tiptoed out of her room, even though we had sworn we would never do that, turning back to have another peek at our girl and grin at each other like kids. Blissfully unaware of the even-greater challenges that were about to unfold before our bleary eyes, I grabbed his hand and scampered off to the bedroom. In pre-Xena days this would naturally have led to an afternoon delight but, for the first time in our love-life, I could safely say that was the last thing on my mind.

❀ ❀ ❀

Our first night at home passed by like a dream. One of those horrible ones from which you are relieved to wake up and realise that what you thought was real was only in your head. But this nightmare was real. Between the hours of 10 pm and 6 am, Xena woke three times. Given our complicated arrangement of feeding with nipple shields, rolled up towels and feeding pillows, I was hardly a prime candidate for feeding her in our bed, so it was out to the armchair in the lounge room at regular intervals. It was a long, lonely and exhausting night. Was anyone else in the world awake or just me?

The reality of newborn nights

You may hit the jackpot and deliver a baby who likes to sleep for long stretches at night from day one, but this would be an exception rather than the norm. The rest of us should expect to feed our newborns three to four times, maybe more, maybe less, between the hours of 7 pm and 7 am.

It's a good idea to make night feeds quieter and calmer then daytime feeds. Keep the lights dim, the noise down and speak in hushed tones. See if you can get away with changing your baby before a

After the third feed, Xena just wouldn't settle. I was almost ready to dump her on the Big Guy, get in the car and drive off in the general direction of the horizon when I remembered the dummy I had bought months earlier—just in case. This was definitely a case of 'just in case'. I ripped the packaging open and was just about to direct it to where it would best fit when a warning bell went off in my head. Um, didn't these things have to be sterilised?

And so I found myself, at 5 am, flicking through the index of my babycare book (the one I never got around to reading) to discover that the potentially life-saving dummy had to either be soaked in antibacterial liquid for an hour, complete a cycle in a sterilising unit or be boiled in a pot of water for five to 10 minutes. So tired that I wanted to throw up, but also desperate for sleep, I had to give it a shot. Juggling Xena with one arm, I boiled up some dummy

Keep it clean, ladies

Popping your baby's dummy into your mouth to 'clean' it actually coats it in another layer of germs—yours! Much better to clean a new or dropped dummy in hot soapy water, a steriliser or the dishwasher and then let it dry before handing it back to bub.

feed, rather than after, as being de-robed and re-nappied tends to wake up even sleepy babies, especially on a chilly night. So, when your baby cries out at night in hunger, change him or her first, then follow with a feed that hopefully leaves bub feeling deliciously content, sleepy and ready to go straight back to bed. In contrast, daytime feeds will naturally be lighter, brighter, noisier and more playful. The idea is that this helps your baby differentiate between day and night, so he or she gradually becomes more wakeful and active during the day, and therefore more inclined to sleep for longer periods throughout the night. Well, that's the theory.

soup, let the dummy cool and then gently pushed it into her mouth. Her little tongue pushed it right back out again. So I pushed it back in. And then she pushed it out. This frustrating game could have gone on all night but then I came up with a brainwave. Even though we'd just fed, I'd feed her again until she fell asleep, swap the breast for a dummy and put her down to bed. Having been up with me for almost an hour, Xena was exhausted and in no position to argue. Mission accomplished, even if it had taken double the time it should have. Tucking her back up in her bed, I realised I had lasted at home for less than 24 hours before succumbing to the lure of a bubba plugger. Was that some kind of record? If it was, I didn't care. I was off to bed.

Dummies for mummies

For some strange reason, dummies tend to provoke intense love or hate reactions among parents. I really don't see what all the fuss is about, and suspect that vocal opponents are just peeved their baby wouldn't take one.

The facts are that giving your baby a dummy can:

- soothe your baby and make him or her happy
- signal sleep time to your baby
- possibly reduce the risk of Sudden Infant Death Syndrome (SIDS)
- be less damaging to teeth than thumb sucking.

On the downside, dummies can cause some problems such as the following:

- Babies may need re-plugging to settle throughout the night.
- A dummy can be thrown from the pram or the cot and get lost or dirty, which can be a nuisance.

- Weaning bub off dummy use can be traumatic.

- If dummy use extends to the toddler years, buying new dummies can become expensive.

- Some experts believe dummies can interfere with breastfeeding.

Just make sure you stock up on dummies or choose a dummy that is readily available, as babies tend to become very attached to a certain shape and style and often reject substitutes.

Chapter 5

Getting *out and about* with baby

The heavens opened and the rain poured down for most of our first week at home. This was probably just as well as we wouldn't have been able to get out even if we'd wanted to, so firmly was I locked in the never-ending cycle of caring for Xena. On a rare trip out the front door—all the way to the letterbox—I found a card from a friend saying, 'Welcome to the world'. Cute, but not quite accurate. We hadn't really managed to take Xena anywhere other than from her bedroom to the lounge room and vice versa since we'd come home.

Family life was not quite as I had imagined. The armchair in the lounge room was now the seat of all action. Visitors would find me there, no matter what time they arrived, pinned down by the baby lying across my lap. They weren't the only ones to pay homage to the chair. Like loyal followers, packets of nappies (hooray, disposables!), wipes and a growing pile of bibs had made their way from the change table in Xena's room to litter the base of the chair. We'd begun by using the change table for every nappy and outfit change, but, after just one day, we got sick of going back and forth between the two rooms before, during and after every feed. If nothing else, breastfeeding was keeping our daughter explosively regular.

I longed to be the confident out-and-about mum I had imagined when I was pregnant, bouncing my bonny baby on my knee while I exchanged hilarious anecdotes with other mums at a barbecue or leisurely cruising the shops with my pram. But the thought of leaving the house was just too stressful. My entire day was spent feeding, changing, feeding, changing, changing, feeding and settling Xena.

While she slept I did a few basic things for myself such as showering, going to the toilet or washing clothes. Then, before I knew it, Xena would wake and the time-consuming

Breastfeeding in public

The thought of lobbing out a boob for a feed in public can be terrifying for a beginner. The first thing you need to know is that you have the legal right to breastfeed anywhere you want to. If anyone tells you to stop or to move somewhere out of view, they clearly need reminding that you're feeding a real, live, hungry baby—not pole dancing for their enjoyment.

Having said that, most mums try to be as discreet as possible and minimise nipple flashing. Here's how you can ensure you're comfortable breastfeeding in public:

- Choose tops with easy feeding access—not a T-shirt that you need to cycle would start all over again. How on earth was I supposed to fit leaving the house into this exhaustive routine, let alone breastfeed in public without showing my supposedly flat nipples to the word? Nope, the world would just have to wait to meet Xena.

Well, everyone would have to wait to meet Xena except Doris, the early childhood nurse down at the local community health centre, who had prompted Xena's first expedition to the world outside our four walls. I had bowed to the substantial pressure in hospital to book an appointment with the nurse for Xena's two-week check-up, and consequently we were due at the clinic at the end of our first week at home. As the day drew closer, I realised that the midwives were pretty switched

Bathroom buddies

You don't need to wait until your baby is asleep to get ready in the morning. Get her used to lying in a rocker nearby while you shower and dress. It won't take her long to become used to this routine and you'll feel more equipped to face the day when you swap the stale PJs for a shower, fresh clothes and a lick of mascara.

hike up to your neck. Some maternity garments are actually designed with clever features that allow low-exposure feeding.

- Take a light baby blanket or muslin wrap to drape over your feeding-side shoulder and your feeding baby.

- Locate the parents' room at your local shopping centre and take your baby there for a feed. Call ahead to check that there's a suitable babycare area at your destination.

- Feed your baby in the car on arrival—this may fill bub up enough to get him or her through your expedition.

- Visit <www.breastfeeding. asn/advocacy/welcome list. asp> to find breast-friendly locations near you.

Ready, set . . .

Try to keep your nappy bag packed and ready to go at all times. Take two minutes at the end of each day to restock a bag with nappies (each in a plastic bag for easy disposal), wipes and a change of clothing. That's one less thing to faff around with when you next have to go out.

on to the new-mum mentality. Had we not made the appointment in hospital, I seriously doubt that the thought of initiating a check-up would have crossed my mind. Far too busy for that, baby.

At 1 am on the morning of our appointment, I began to nut out our action plan. Naturally I was also feeding Xena at the time. If she next fed at 4 am and then again at 7 am, we were stuffed because she'd need feeding just before we had to leave for the clinic and we'd miss our appointment. I'd have to either get to the clinic half an hour earlier to feed her before we saw the nurse or try to bring the 7 am feed forward. Oh, the logistics of it all.

Of course Xena ended up sleeping longer than I had anticipated (hooray!), and I ended up having to rework the schedule again at 5 am. But by then, Plan B wasn't looking so crash-hot either. Xena's 5 am feed would probably be followed by another at about 8 am, I calculated, and then we'd be stuffed again because she'd be sound asleep when we were due at the clinic. And appointment or no appointment, I was not prepared to break the 11th commandment: thou shalt not waketh thy sleeping baby. In the end, Xena did the complete opposite of what I had expected anyway, sleeping until 9 am, which conveniently gave me time

Don't sweat the details

The easiest way to get out and about with a baby is to avoid micro-managing it. Just commit to the outing and deal with the logistics on the day. Trying to anticipate how feeds and sleeps might fit in will only mess with your head—and it will never pan out that way, anyway.

to shower and dress. A quick feed later and, finally, after seven days of self-imposed exile, the three of us set foot outside the front door to brave the great unknown—our first family outing.

The two-week check-up

The Big Guy carried Xena into the community centre, where we took our place among the other nervous-looking bodies in the waiting room. Out of the corner of my eye, I checked out other parents checking out other parents out of the corner of their eyes. What were we all looking for? Signs of cracking? Evidence that some were coping better than others? Friends? Foes? Allies? Nope, probably more like who had the most expensive pram. Where did people get the money for these things? Was there another baby bonus we didn't qualify for? A designer pram allowance, perhaps?

Shop talk

If you're tempted to pay four-figure sums of money for baby gear, pinch yourself out of your stupor, identify a more basic model that you could happily live with and buy it. Next, take the difference and spend it on a cleaner for the next six to 12 months. This will bring you much more joy.

On the walls and shelves was a former rainforest of literature targeting novice parents like me. *Immunisation. Breastfeeding. Postnatal depression. Infant massage. Nappy rash. Development stages. First solid foods for baby.* Diligently I collected every leaflet and flyer, except for anything that had a picture of an older child or toddler on the front because I just couldn't imagine Xena ever growing out of babyhood. But the baby information was a must-have, to be taken home and filed in the brand-new lever arch folder I had bought to store such useful pieces of information.

Tucking the pamphlets into the side pocket of the nappy bag, I wasn't to know that the pamphlets—let alone the lever arch system—would never again see the light of day. My intentions were good, and that was all that counted.

The door to a cubicle-sized office opened, revealing a smart but casually dressed woman of grandmotherly age. She looked friendly and kind, which made me hope she was our appointed nurse. But alas—she called out an unfamiliar surname, prompting the couple next to us to propel their baby's outrageously flashy set of wheels into her office. Five minutes later, a plump middle-aged woman with fuzzy hair and an over-the-top 'I'm-having-fun-here-even-if-it-kills-me' grin poked her head out from behind another door. 'Ten bucks says she's our Doris', I whispered to the Big Guy.

'Hello, Mum, Dad', she beamed in our general direction, gesturing with her index finger for us to make our way over to her. After first checking that Doris's parents weren't behind us, I realised that we were the mum and dad she had referred to. There was no choice but to heed the finger and make our way over to her room. 'And this must be Xelda!'

'It's Xena', I corrected, once we were seated behind her closed door. 'You know, like the warrior princess, minus the weapons of deadly destruction.' No, actually, she didn't know. 'How very [pause] unusual', replied Doris. And had we brought Xena's blue book? We handed over the child health record presented to us in hospital, and as she flicked through to the first clinic check-up page Doris stopped to smile at our daughter and tell us what we both knew: 'She's a beauty'.

Then came crunch time: 'How's it all going? How's feeding?'

'We-ell, I'm trying my hardest, but I don't think we're very good at it', I answered honestly, trying to deflect some of the blame onto Xena in a bid to make the problem seem more widespread than just my own inadequacy. 'In fact, now that you mention it, I'm not quite sure that breastfeeding is working for us. And to top it off I feel like the walking dead because I don't get much sleep.' The beaming smile slipped off Doris's face. Great, I thought. She's going to say, 'Right you are, it's not working, time to try something else'. Not quite. The first thing she said when she regained composure was: 'You shouldn't be tired. Don't you sleep when your baby sleeps?' Dumbly, I shook my head. 'You mums today,' she began, collectively lumping me in with a whole lot of women I didn't know, 'should stop trying to do the supermum thing. And get yourself a can of this', she added, scrawling the name of a powdered supplement on a scrap of paper. 'It'll give you more energy.' I couldn't quite believe what I was hearing. Didn't this woman know what life was like with a newborn? And if not, why was she in a position to be our adviser? Far from trying to be supermum, I was simply trying to get through daily life with my baby. She could keep her energy in a can. What I needed was sleep — in the can, in the laundry, anywhere. (I was hardly in a position to be fussy.)

And now, she continued, what exactly was our problem with feeding?

My goodness, where should we begin? Should I tell her that I was sick of trying to make silicone function like skin? That I couldn't find a comfortable and workable position? How my breasts were still so full that milk squirted every which way, turning my breast into a slip-and-slide fun park for the shield? Should I say what I'd been thinking for the past seven days, that maybe Xena wasn't getting enough milk? Should I confess that I had fantasised about buying a tin of formula?

No, I probably shouldn't so I didn't. Instead I mumbled something innocuous about the nipple shield being 'a bit of a hassle'. 'Hang in there Mum', said Doris. 'By six weeks you'll be fine.' Xena looked pretty good, she said, and we'd check her out just as soon as we'd gone through the rest of the paperwork. Oh yes, and I might want to think about joining one of the mothers' groups she'd organised for women in our local area. Then again, I might not, I thought belligerently. The last thing I wanted was to socialise with a gaggle of other mums who were probably all coping much better than me.

In the meantime, Doris had arrived at the section in the blue book that had questions I was supposed to have answered in preparation for the first clinic visit. Aside

Coping with mum envy

Remember looking at the popular girls in high school and thinking they were so much more together than you? A similarly destructive thought has been known to plague new mothers who start believing that every other mum is handling the mother-load more successfully, happily and easily than they are. Ridiculous, isn't it? You'd think we'd have learnt to leave all that nonsense back in the schoolyard where it belongs.

The truth is that even the poster mums who make it look so easy will have days when they want to disappear under a doona because it's all too hard, they're fed up from the 'before your baby's first health check' questions there was a newborn-to-nine-months safety questionnaire, both of which I had completely overlooked. 'No problem,' said Doris, with the merest hint of disapproval, 'we can run through them verbally'. Did Xena travel in an approved car restraint? Yes, the Big Guy and I both loved the colour; that's why we bought it. Did I leave Xena alone in the car? No, but the thought was tempting at times. Did I stay with my baby when she was in the bath, even if the phone rang? Absolutely, especially when it was Great Aunty Mavis calling with her haemorrhoid update — that was one call I was happy to let go to voicemail.

As Doris travelled down the list, I was forced to become a little, er, creative in my responses. Which basically meant I lied to save face. I told her that no, I didn't drink hot drinks when my baby was in my arms, even though I always slurped a cup of tea while Xena slurped me. And I answered that, yes, I had removed all ribbons and ties from my baby's

and everything has gone wrong.

So don't kid yourself that you're the only one struggling to cope, and do nurture yourself by:

- resting when your baby sleeps, at least for the first few weeks

- talking about how you are feeling to your partner, friends or family — you may well discover others in the same boat

- not leaving people guessing about what help and support you need — tell it like it is

- doing something for yourself every day such as listen to your favourite music, paint your toenails, read a few pages of a book or do whatever makes you feel like you again.

clothing and checked that the spaces between the rails of the cot were between 50 millimetres and 80 millimetres wide, even though I wouldn't have thought to do either in a million years. But the last question was the doozy: had I disposed of all large sheets of plastic in the house and knotted plastic bags for storage or disposal? 'You'd better believe it', I told Doris. Surely that wasn't a lie as such?

With the checklist completed, it was time for Doris to check out Xena herself. Doris measured her length and head circumference before we stripped her bare for a weigh-in that revealed Xena hadn't gained any weight since we left hospital one week ago. In fact, she'd lost 50 grams. 'Nothing to worry about', said Doris, a little too brightly. 'But I do suggest you make an appointment with the lactation consultant at your hospital fairly soon. As in, immediately. And keep up the feeding, Mum!'

Keep up the feeding? No, Doris, I thought I'd let my two-week-old daughter fend for herself.

Walking back out to the car, I had that disconcerting feeling I remembered from years ago, when I knew I was bringing home a bad report card from school. My grades were poor and I'd failed to demonstrate a sound grasp of the year's major project. In fact, my work was going backwards, not forwards. In my frazzled, delusional state, I was convinced that the hieroglyphics Doris scrawled in the blue book read along the following lines: Xena's mum is not working to her full potential and should apply herself more to the task at hand. With additional tutoring, there is every chance she could achieve a reasonable grade.

In other words: pull your socks up, lovey.

Chapter 6

Making a boob of
breastfeeding

Exactly three weeks after Xena's birth, I found myself back at the hospital to visit the head hooters honcho (the Big Guy's words, not mine). Despite the fact that I did precious little other than sit in our once-best-but-now-least-favourite puke-stained armchair and feed, feed, feed around the clock in marathon sessions (well, that's what they felt like from where I was sitting) Xena still wasn't putting on weight. The really odd thing was that my udders were chock-full of milk. If I could have chopped them off and weighed each one, I would not have been surprised to discover they were a couple of kilos each, judging by their heft. At every feed, I experienced that dragging sensation of 'let-down' that told me my milk was making its way down from wherever it originated to Xena's hungry mouth. And Xena herself looked healthy enough to my inexperienced eye. She was still a strong little thing, with a round face and inquisitive eyes that seemed to know a little too much—like maybe that her mother was a bit of a joke, especially since the woman couldn't even manage to put enough juice in her wee belly for her to stack on some kilos. Grams, even. I was, apparently, so hopeless that we had to call in the experts. Consultation of the lactation variety was the key to helping Xena thrive, according to Doris the health nurse. Silly me, and I just thought she needed a decent feed.

The consultant was nice enough, dwarfed as she was by enormous images of dissected bosoms showing industrial-sized veins, milk ducts and areola. 'Sounds like a pasta sauce, don't you think?' I chuckled, pointing to the areola on the nearest poster to try to lighten the mood. But to no avail. Time was mammaries, and mammaries with milk were mammaries on a mission. My frivolity was irresponsibly depriving Xena of precious grams of body mass. We cut out the pleasantries and got down to business.

Weighty matters

Many parents freak out when their baby isn't putting on enough weight according to the growth charts in their health record book and are tempted to fatten bub up with formula because 'at least you know how much bub's drinking'. But these growth charts are by no means definitive—in fact, their accuracy is currently being questioned by some experts. Apparently, the charts are based largely on babies born in the US during the 1970s, when formula feeding was more the norm. Consequently, the WHO recently issued revised versions based on

The consultant scribbled away on her notepad as I filled her in on why we were sitting inside her stuffy little office on such a glorious autumn day. I started with Xena's weight loss and worked backwards, outlining the nipple shield, jaundice, supply line feeding set-up and Xena's long-term reluctance to feed. At the end of the story the consultant said exactly what I was expecting: 'Let's see her in action'.

Trying hard to exude casual confidence, I unbuttoned my shirt and retrieved a freshly sterilised nipple shield from an equally sterile container in the nappy bag. Feeding Xena in the privacy of my own home was stressful enough, but feeding on demand in a strange room was actually quite traumatic. Longing for my big fat armchair, I did the best I could with a plastic-covered pillow, a chair without arms and a silent plea to Xena to give it her best shot. I just wanted to do the deed and get out of there, back to the safety of my home, where no-one could see me stuff up or freak me out with cross-sections of giant boobs.

Xena did her strange 'I'm a wet dog shaking myself dry' thing with her head for a few minutes, skimming her

breastfed babies, which you can find at <www.who.int/childgrowth>.

While the experts thrash out which charts are more relevant to Aussie babes, bear in mind the other indicators of a thriving baby:

- feeding well throughout the day
- lots of wet and dirty nappies
- usually settles well after a feed
- alert and interested when awake.

Genetics also play a part in your baby's size and weight gain, so ask your parents if you or your partner were skinny babies before you push the panic buttons.

Leaks and let-down

Let-down is the physical sensation you feel deep within your breasts when your milk starts flowing from the storage ducts to your nipple. Some women describe it as a dragging feeling, others experience sensations of fullness, cramping or tingling, as well as dripping and spraying. Let-down can be triggered when your baby starts feeding. You may also experience let-down and the subsequent involuntary leakage at other times, namely when your baby sleeps through a feed, when you are away from your baby and start to think about him or her or when you

mouth across the shield without making serious contact. We probably could have continued like that all day had the consultant not decided to give my girl a hand. Gripping the back of her head with her hand, she propelled Xena's face down onto my breast, mashing her nose against my skin in the process. Jeez, I hated that move. It may have achieved its aim of latching her on, but boy it looked brutal.

The consultant peered down to check out Xena's form. Her little cheeks pulsed in and out as she drank steadily for several minutes. After walking around to check out the action from all sides, the consultant sat back down in her chair and declared that she couldn't see a problem. I obviously had a good supply of milk, judging by the mess we'd made in a few minutes, she said. And the attachment seemed fine. As for the shield, well, it wasn't the best way to go but if it got the job done, then we should stick with it until I was confident to try bare breast again. 'Nope, all's well', she declared happily before dropping the clanger: 'But I do suggest you give her a top-up 10 or 20 minutes hear another baby cry. So don't be surprised to suddenly find yourself looking like a contestant in a wet T-shirt competition when you least expect it. Unexpected let-down leakage should settle down when your body becomes more used to your baby's feeding patterns, usually in the second month. In the meantime:

- wear breast pads in between feeds
- wear clothes that camouflage leaks
- keep a spare shirt and bra in your nappy bag or the car, just in case you have a major flood when you are out and about
- fold your arms tightly across your chest to stop the flow.

after each feed and express milk between feeds to boost your supply even further'.

Top-ups? Expressing more milk to give her in between already ridiculously frequent feeds? Was boob woman out of her mind? Did she really think I had the time, energy or inclination to triple my breastfeeding workload? Because that's what her suggestion would amount to. More feeds, more self-milking, less life. No, no, no. I didn't want to play this game anymore. Something had to give, and it wasn't going to be my tenuous hold on my sanity.

'Er, couldn't we just give her one or two feeds of formula throughout the day?' I ventured. 'Just to see if it will help her put on some weight and also well, you know, to give me a bit of a break because I really don't think I can do this for much longer ...' I petered off, and dared to look up from my poor little Xena, the oblivious cause of her mother's growing sense of anxiety and panic.

'Good heavens, no! Why on *earth* would you want to do *that*?' boob woman exploded. 'The beginning of formula is also the end of breastfeeding', she warned darkly. And her problem was?

'It really is worth the effort to persevere', she said. 'You'd kick yourself in the long run for depriving your precious little one of all that goodness, just to make things a little easier for you now. Come back and see me again in two weeks, just to check all's going well.'

Holding back tears, I hoisted Xena over one shoulder and the nappy bag over the other. It was nowhere near feeding time, but I was suddenly overwhelmed by a different kind of let-down feeling; one that had nothing to do with my breasts.

We were two streets away from home when I did a quick U-turn and headed back towards the local supermarket. Five minutes later I was standing in the baby aisle, clutching Xena and eyeing off the tins of formula. The names, numbers and ingredients on the labels read like a secret code that was impossible to crack. Choosing an engine oil would have been easier, and I knew even less about cars than I did about babies.

Why the dire warnings about formula?

Put it this way: if you mix the wrong amount of formula with unclean water in dirty bottles, your baby may become ill. If, on the other hand, you are a responsible adult who follows the simple instructions for making and giving formula, your baby will thrive—much like his or her breastfed counterparts. There's really nothing to be afraid of.

I must have reached for three different tins and then changed my mind each time, swayed by more important-sounding names or ingredients, or even the colours on the packaging. When I finally thought I had earmarked a type suitable for babies from birth, I read the back of the tin and lost my resolve. 'Breastmilk is best for your baby ... Infant formula is not intended to replace breastmilk ...' Hello? What was it intended to replace? Coffee?

Combining breast milk and formula feeds

Supplementing breastfeeds with some formula feeds seems like an obvious choice for many women, but it tends to be frowned on by breastfeeding experts for the following reasons:

- Introducing a bottle to a breastfed baby may cause 'nipple confusion', which could make bub forget how to feed from a breast after feeding from a bottle.

- Your baby may start to prefer feeding from a bottle as it's less work than feeding from a breast.

- Replacing breastfeeds with formula will reduce the amount of breast milk your body produces.

The main concern about feeding formula to your baby is that any or all of these factors may ultimately make breastfeeding more challenging, and may therefore influence a mother to quit breastfeeding altogether. That's not to say it can't be done, especially if an occasional bottle of formula will give you the break you need to breastfeed for longer. You just need to take it slowly and carefully. Consider doing the following things to reduce the impact of formula top-ups on your ability to breastfeed:

- Wait until your breastmilk supply is established before using formula. This should be around six weeks.

- Never mix formula with breast milk. Instead, feed your baby breastmilk first and then top up with a bottle of formula.

- Keep formula feeds occasional so you don't affect your breastmilk supply.

The warnings continued: 'Incorrect administering can harm your baby ... Seek medical advice before feeding your baby this scary stuff, you horrible woman'. Clearly, feeding formula to Xena was the worst thing I could do. Pushing the tin back onto the shelf, I bolted out of the store.

Chapter 7

Getting to know your baby

When she was four weeks old, Xena smiled at me. When I told everyone, I knew what they were thinking, but they were all wrong: Xena's smile wasn't just 'wind'. All the books said to expect the first smile from six weeks, and nothing but the visual effects of a windy stomach before then. But nope, at four weeks of age, my daughter smiled at me and me only. Her timing was immaculate, coinciding with my feeling of despair about the fact that my life now resembled one big nipple shield and was totally devoid of sleep—not necessarily in that order.

It happened at around 1 am, interrupting a sweet dream of pre-baby days, when there was just the Big Guy, me and time on our sides—time to do what we wanted, when we wanted; time to kill, doing nothing else but sleeping away an entire day if we felt so inclined. My reverie was broken by that all-too-familiar cry of 'I'm awake and by George I'm famished'. As usual, it took a few minutes to anchor the cries to reality and register that this was my cue to put my own needs on hold to attend to Xena's.

Dragging myself into her room, I switched on the night-light and leaned into the cot to pick her up, when there it was in all its glory: an uneven, gummy grin punctuated by a tiny pink tongue darting in and out in time with her arms and legs flapping excitedly at her sides. My mood was broken. It may have been the wee hours of the morning, and I may have had a gutful of 24/7 duty, but that smile gave me hope. It was the first sign that things would change in our relationship; that it wouldn't always be about me giving, giving, giving and her taking, taking and then taking some more. That smile was more than just a smile; it was my daughter saying, 'Sorry, Mum, I know it's hard going but hang in there. Here's a little of what you can expect further down the track [insert grin here] and have I shown you today how devastatingly cute I am?'

She really was gorgeous. Her outlandish Uncle Otto–esque mullet had seemingly disappeared overnight (thank goodness), and had been replaced by a soft cap of baby-fine hair that cradled her beautifully rounded head. She wasn't all skin and bone, nor was she plump. Rather, she was both strong and soft all at the same time.

But, truth be told, this girl was not at all what I had expected a daughter of mine to look like. Even after several weeks of ownership, every time I looked at her I got a shock at the unfamiliar face staring right back at me. Had I been expecting a mini me, perhaps? Someone as recognisable as my own baby photos? Possibly a Huggies ad baby?

Aha! Maybe that was it! I had been conditioned by media babies. Flawless infants who seemed to skip the labour-intensive newborn stage and arrive into the world sitting, crawling, clapping hands or taking first tentative steps, all the while making impossibly sweet babbling sounds and grinning endlessly at their doting mums. And mine didn't match up — no wonder I didn't recognise her!

My baby, in contrast, was a determined little body, cranky as all get-out at times and prone to impatience. At the beginning of most feeds, for instance, she could hardly contain herself, opening her mouth enormously wide and flinging her head from side to side in a frenzied attempt to latch on. When I attempted to help her out by stopping her wet dog–shaking routine and directing her to the source of her meal, she would howl furiously until she was actually conscious of the feel of the nipple shield in her mouth. With a 'why didn't you do this in the first place?' kind of grunt, she'd suck away, pausing every now and then to tense her tummy, burp or fart before starting all over again. If I wasn't satisfied she'd fed for long enough (which was every other feed) and tried to encourage her to take more, she would simply lie there with her little lips pursed tightly and refuse to cooperate further. No amount of dripping milk on her lips or teasing her mouth with a full breast would make her change her mind.

Cranky babies

Physical discomfort from common infant conditions such as reflux or even the after-effect of a difficult or long birth have all been known to affect a baby's temperament. If your baby always seems unsettled or cranky, have her examined by your GP or paediatrician to rule out a medical cause.

Her determination extended into tummy time, making this a miserable exercise for both of us. Every day saw me attempt to clock up the recommended half an hour of floor time, placing Xena on her tummy on a rug. Every day saw Xena lift her head up for a few seconds and then let out an indignant howl, sobbing into the rug. Every day it would take about 30 seconds before I'd crack and flip her over onto her back. This was an equally unpopular move, and pretty soon after I would abandon any pretence of trying to encourage Xena's physical development and carry her around for a while, which, of course, had been her preferred outcome all along. The other possibility was to lie her in the rocker for a few minutes—a few minutes was about as much as she could cope with—and let her soak up her surroundings. I loved it when she was happy enough to lie like this, largely because she did it with such style. With her ankles crossed and both fists

Mirror, mirror

Babies love looking at faces, especially ones like their own. One must-have toy that you'll use from early on is a soft-edged baby mirror that you can place in front of your bub to keep him amused during tummy time and to hold and smooch when he or she gets a little older.

Tummy time

Placing your baby on her tummy on the floor is recommended in the first two months in order to help her build strength in the muscles that allow her to hold up her head without your help. Unfortunately, lots of new babies absolutely hate this developmental exercise because it's just too much hard work. (Incidentally, the babies who hate being on their tummies are the ones that need to practise the most—or so the theory goes.) The trick is to start with very short sessions—just resting under her chin, she'd peer up at me through enormous blinking eyes. Usually I'd offer her her favourite dummy, which she'd almost vacuum out of my hands before it even reached her lips. Once firmly in position, the dummy would bob up and down frantically in time with the rhythm of her sucking.

But the peace was always short-lived. I think I once drank a cup of tea in the time she was happy in the rocker, but I could have been mistaken. Anyway, odds were I'd never be able to read *War and Peace* while Xena whiled away the hours in the rocker.

Although her traits and some behaviours were becoming more familiar by the day, I still found it hard to describe Xena when asked about her, especially in relation to that awful question: is she a good baby? To me, an ideal baby would feed, settle and change itself during the hours of nine and five and sleep soundly from 6 pm through to 8 am. A 'good' baby would be a couple of steps down from that in the self-sufficiency department. Xena did none of

30 or 60 seconds at a time—and build up to longer periods of tummy time. You can help make it more enjoyable (if that's possible) for your baby by:

- placing a rolled-up towel under your baby's chest so that bub's slightly raised and less inclined to face-plant the floor

- getting down on the floor with your baby, so she can see you

- putting some toys in front of your baby

- using a colourful play mat with bits and bobs for your baby to explore while she is on her tummy.

those things: she ran me ragged with feeding and nappy changes during the day, was sometimes hard to settle and at other times went to sleep without much fuss. Sometimes she slept for two or three hours; at other times she slept for half an hour. But I loved her madly and when she smiled, I melted. Were these the characteristics of a 'good' baby? How on earth would I have known?

Perhaps the question should have been, 'How good are you, as a mum, at dealing with your baby's enigmatic ways?' And my answer to that would have varied depending on whether I was feeling incredibly blessed to have my daughter or rather inclined to give her away for a few days.

How to entertain a newborn

That room full of toys and the expensive baby gym may not be as appealing to your new baby as you had imagined. And all those parents who declared that 'you absolutely *must* have a baby swing, activity table or set of blocks' were referring to a time in the not-too-distant-future—many weeks, if not months, away—when your little one might actually be capable of enjoying them for a few minutes at a time. In the first few weeks and months, bub's awake time is best spent having close cuddles with you talking goo goo ga ga, grabbing your thumb and trying to ram it into his mouth, or taking in the scenery from the comfort of the pram, baby sling, reclining chair or rocker or your arms. Bub may also enjoy lying in his or her rocker or lying on a blanket placed so he or she can gaze at:

- a moving mobile
- wind chimes
- trees blowing in the wind
- hanging moving objects such as clothes on the line or balloons tied to a branch of a tree.

Nature or nurture? Where your baby's personality comes from

It's fair to say your baby is a mixture of personality traits he or she inherited and learned from parents and home life—a combination of nature and nurture.

Some factors that influence your baby's personality include:

- *genetics*. Your baby inherits certain personality traits from her parents.

- *your vibes*. Babies pick up on feelings of calmness and happiness, as well as stress and anxiety from their parents.

- *home life*. A calm environment and happy household gives your baby a sense of security, which can affect her personality.

- *gender*. Although this is generally more evident in the toddler/preschooler years, your baby's gender may influence how people care for him or her.

- *position in the family*. A firstborn child is generally perceived to be more anxious than subsequent siblings.

- *your pregnancy*. Apparently, there is a link between stressed mums-to-be and unsettled babies.

- *astrology*. If you believe in this sort of thing, look up your baby's star sign. This will provide you with a less-scientific insight into what makes your baby tick.

Chapter 8

Desperately seeking *support*

Five weeks into this new gig and, at the Big Guy's insistence, I dragged myself along to the next mothers' group meeting for new mums in my area. My guess is that he was starting to worry about me, because for once in my life I was having trouble relating to my peers. Childless friends were suddenly on the outer, purely because they evoked too much envy. They had freedom, personal time and unlimited potential to sleep—all of which I craved. And besides, they weren't overly interested in Xena—understandably—whereas I was unable to put her out of my mind. On the rare occasions when the Big Guy and I entertained or went out with her, I fretted endlessly that she might need a feed, sleep or cardigan. On the even rarer occasions when we entertained or went out without her, I had problems trying to fight back the urge to Xena-ise every conversation.

'Oh really, Phil? You've just been to France? How interesting. You know, we thought about calling Xena "Paris", but couldn't agree on the spelling.'

'Yes, I'm sure your navel piercing was very painful, Jo. And have I told you about my episiotomy?'

And that's about as far as any such conversation would go because suddenly the person I'd cornered had to urgently visit the bathroom, refresh their drink or make a quick call to a long-lost cousin. Strange that this always happened just as I came to the bit about the cut to my nether regions.

Hello world, remember me?

It's easy to get so absorbed by what's going on inside your four walls that you start to ignore the invigorating world just outside. The best thing to do when you are feeling overwhelmed is to change your scenery. A walk, a dose of fresh air and just saying hello to a passerby can help make you feel connected to that world again.

Other friends with older babies or children would have welcomed me happily to their social club, but I didn't feel I qualified to become a member just yet. They all looked so content and in control, laughing off their latest child-related catastrophe or talking right over the crying babies they jiggled on their hips, whereas I was still stumbling around in a daze. I may have held down responsible jobs, backpacked all over the world and mastered the art of a DIY bikini wax in my pre-baby life, but motherhood was more stressful and—dare I say it—equally painful at times.

Secretly I hoped the Big Guy was right about going along to mothers' group. Perhaps this was where I would find a like-minded soul.

Feeling isolated? You're not alone

In those first few feet-finding months of being a mum, when your days revolve around caring for your baby and your contact with the outside world is limited (or compromised by your inability to talk about anything non-baby related), it's normal to feel isolated and even lonely at times. The good news is that this stage will be over before you know it, as hard as that is to imagine right now. In the meantime, you can make life feel a little friendlier by:

- making regular contact with sympathetic friends, family and neighbours who you can count on for a chat, a chuckle or even a cry if need be

- listening to talkback radio, especially if you are geographically isolated, to remind yourself that there is life beyond your baby (and that you may reconnect with it one day soon)

- SMS-ing friends when you sit down to feed your baby

- signing up to an online mothers' forum or chat room

- frequenting the same cafe, supermarket or newsagent, so you get to know the staff and vice versa.

I'd almost chickened out of the mothers' group meeting, unenthused about having to get myself and Xena down to the local community centre at 10 am for the sake of socialising when I could have used the time much more productively. Sterilising a batch of nipple shields, for instance, immediately sprang to mind. Also, I was feeling a wee bit shy. The group I was to join had been established a few weeks earlier. Most likely they had already bonded, sharing intimate confidences about pooing in the throes of labour and laughing about how they all vowed to cut off their husband's testicles so they would never see the inside of a delivery suite again. I already felt like a stranger in a foreign land; I didn't feel up to being the new girl in a room full of lactating bosom buddies. Although, as Doris the health nurse had taken great pains to point out, I would be attending a parents' group, not a mothers' group. Dads were more than welcome too, she'd said, which was great in theory, but when I walked into the room of women at exactly 10.07 am that Wednesday morning, I discovered it was nothing more than political correctness in our instance.

Doris was holding court when I arrived, having arranged to screen a video on settling recalcitrant babies for this meeting. 'Hello there, Mum', she called out cheerfully, and in doing so turned every head in the room. If she couldn't remember our names, perhaps she should allocate us numbers: Mum One, Mum Two and so on. Parking Xena next to the nearest vacant seat, I sat down and sized up the room. All up there were 12 other mums in the group, each with a reasonably brand-new baby in a brand-spanking-new pram, the likes of which the Big Guy and I had vetoed purely because those four-wheeled babies cost more than my weekly salary. That would be the salary I no longer received, of course.

Eleven of the faces were new, but one looked vaguely familiar. It took a few seconds and the sound of the familiar woman's piercing voice to recognise one of my former roommates in hospital. Oh crikey, I hoped she'd locked up her wayward man and his stabbing friends someplace safe, because I certainly didn't want them roaming the streets while I was out with my baby. She glanced up at me in recognition and quickly looked away, too. Good call chickadee, we'd both play dumb. You don't mention my nightly sob sessions or flat nipples and I won't mention the flesh wound incident.

I turned away from my former inmate to look elsewhere for a new best friend. Ms Matching Teddy Bear Pram and Nappy Bag was out, that was for sure. And I was fairly confident I'd steer clear of Ms I've Stuck Every Conceivable Toy Attachment On The Pram Of My Newborn Who Can't Possibly Make Sense Of It All Yet, and Ms Note Taker. Even my untrained eye could tell they were taking it all a little too seriously. Potential allies included Ms Asked Her Neighbour If She Could Borrow Some Wipes (she forgot hers) and Ms Other New Girl, purely because we were in the same boat and she looked as awkward as I did. For a brief moment I wondered what the other mums thought of me at face value. I'd done my valiant best to scrub up with a lick of paint on my lashes and was fairly sure I'd wiped all the chuck off my shoulder before I left the house. For all intents and purposes, I looked just like any other mum in the room—minus the millionaire's pram. But I was certain my body language would betray me. Couldn't they all feel the vibes I was sending about ditching mumsy chat sessions in a daggy old hall and meeting up like the former crazy young things we once were at the pub over a cold sauv blanc or two? I certainly hoped so.

Speaking of drinking, I desperately wanted to talk to Ms Bottle Feeder. That would have to wait, however, because suddenly Doris was clapping her hands and calling for

Keep it real

There's much to be said for sharing your experiences—good and bad—with other mums. Being honest about your bad days, as well as sharing tips about your good days, will establish a culture of trust and mutual support with other mums, and (hopefully) banish competitive parenting syndrome.

our attention. The chatting stopped abruptly, and we all took our places, rocking prams back and forth or patting babes in arms. Doris got the ball rolling by asking us to quickly go around the room and introduce ourselves. For the benefit of the new mums and a memory jog for the existing group, we were to give our names, our baby's name and age, and explain why we had decided to attend this mothers' — oops, *parents*! — group. By the time she came around to me, I'd met Sophie ('I'm here so my eight-week-old son Damon can meet other kids his age and make lifelong friends'), Jacqui ('None of my friends have babies, so they don't understand what I'm going through') and Joanne ('I just *lurrrve* being a mum and want to talk to other mums about how great it is'). No surprises that Sophie was also the proud owner of the toymobile and Joanne was responsible for the ghastly teddy bear ensemble. There was every chance she also had the matching rocker, port-a-cot and quilt set at home. Helen ('I joined up because I'm craving adult

Could it be PND?

It's a common misconception that mothers who develop postnatal depression (PND) have no tender feelings for their baby or haven't bonded with them. You can love your baby to bits and still have PND. The Edinburgh checklist is used to assess your likelihood of this increasingly common condition. You can find this list at <www.beyondblue.org.au>. Just remember to answer honestly. In the meantime, some of the warning signs of PND include:

- lack of motivation, interest and enjoyment in life generally
- low self-esteem and lack of confidence

company') and Lucy ('I'm here for moral support') were both looking good. And then suddenly, all eyes were on me.

After introducing myself and Xena, I said the first thing that came to my head. 'My husband made me come today because he thinks I've gone psycho, but I came because I need to find other women who aren't finding this a breeze.' Possibly because of my new girl status (but more likely because of the hint of desperation in my voice) Doris honed in on my comments and asked me a few more questions, most of which I suspected were intended to ascertain whether I was a candidate for postnatal depression.

- loss of appetite
- insomnia or difficulty sleeping, even when you have the opportunity
- feeling like you are hopeless, incompetent and unable to cope
- wishing you weren't alive or specific thoughts of suicide
- feeling panicky and anxious
- poor concentration, loss of memory or feelings of being on 'autopilot'
- being irritable and stressed, and being angry with your family
- constantly worrying or obsessing over small things.

If this sounds like you, see your GP for advice about treatment as soon as possible.

After Doris was satisfied that I wasn't about to do horrible things to myself or my baby, she switched on a video about settling sleepless babies. It was full of loads of new and improved advice for mothers of unsettled babies. Not! Actually it was the same ol' same ol' that I'd been trying for weeks and simply hadn't worked. Breastfeed, nappy change, top-up feed and then rewrap your baby.

If all else fails, breastfeed again. Breastfeed, breastfeed, breast-feed until your stupid boobs fall off, and by then your baby should go straight onto a training cup because heaven forbid the introduction of a bottle. Oh yes, and following all that fabulous breastfeeding your baby will sleep soundly day and night. The end, full stop.

> ## What about me?
>
> If you're satisfied you *don't* have PND but still feel as though you're going slightly barmy looking after your baby all the time, make sure you get some me time. Leave bub with your partner once a day or week — whatever you can manage — and take yourself off to see a movie, hit the gym or just be alone to reclaim your headspace.

By the time the credits started to roll, my eyes had also started to roll — towards the back of my head. And Xena was fast asleep in her pram, proving that the drone of that tedious video, if not the advice, really did help to settle recalcitrant babies. Funny that she wouldn't sleep for very long at home but would frequently conk out for an hour or two in her pram in the middle of a strange and noisy environment. Just another one of her quirky little ways to mess with my mind, I decided.

Most of the mums stayed glued to their chairs, now arranged in a circle, while they started to feed their babies. The more adventurous ones placed their babies on their tummies and then bobbed up and down from their chairs to rescue their rug rat when the novelty wore off and the grizzles set in. I left them to it and sought out Ms Bottle Feeder, who was talking intently to Doris. When they broke away I introduced myself and Xena again, gingerly asking how she was going with her new baby. Judging by my experiences, it seemed to be the thing to do.

Modern mothers' groups

If the idea of a traditional mothers' group doesn't float your boat, why not create a social group that's more to your liking? It could be kid-friendly or kid-free depending on whether you feel the need for some space of your own. Some ideas include:

- *book club.* Yes, it may be a challenge reading a whole book in a set period of time, but think of the mental stimulation it will bring.

- *scrapbooking club.* It's not as if you *won't* have enough baby photos to use as material, and you can create family archives and gifts for rellies at the same time.

- *swim club.* Hit the beach or local pool with a group of mums and bubs. Each mum takes turns minding the babies while the others swim laps. Great for developing fitness and friendships.

- *domestic blitz club.* The group of new mums rocks up to one house per week to complete a DIY project or domestic chores. Each mum takes turns minding the babies while the others get the job done.

- *stroller-cise group.* Walk, talk and make friends at the same time.

- *group personal trainer.* Chip in with other mums to hire a boot camp leader to put you through your paces.

I wasn't prepared for the answer, which had nothing to do with how she was going and everything to do with justifying the bottle in the side pocket of her nappy bag. She wished more than anything else in the world to be able to breastfeed. She felt she was doing her baby an injustice by feeding him formula. She believed she had no choice in the matter given her son's horrendous reflux and her paediatrician's strong recommendation of a specialised formula, only available on prescription. 'If I could change one thing in my life I would be able to breastfeed my boy', she assured me earnestly. 'You don't know how lucky you are.' The woman could finally breathe easy that her son wasn't going to choke on his own reflux, but now guilt was choking her.

I tried Big Guy, I honestly did. And then I made a hasty retreat with the pram, walking out the door never to return.

Chapter 9

Coping with *sleep deprivation*

Somehow I muddled through the first six weeks of servitude to Princess Xena, only pausing every now and again to look over my shoulder and watch out for Xena's real mum to appear—the one who would know what she was doing. Still no sign of that elusive woman, so I bumbled along with a lot of guessing, a little help from the Big Guy (when he wasn't at work) and an unhealthy diet of really bad daytime TV.

I had achieved some minor gains. I was now able to take Xena to the shops to pick up emergency supplies instead of dialling the Big Guy at work to place a home-delivery order. I'd made an appointment to get my hair trimmed, actually orchestrated feeds and sleeps to get there on time, and enjoyed a sensational head massage and 40 minutes of pampering while Xena slept soundly in the capsule beside me. And on one extraordinary day I managed to prepare the ingredients for a stir-fry by 5 pm and hang the washing on the line, with Xena hanging placidly from my baby pouch. My poor back would always remember that day, too.

Despite these achievements, I found myself in a difficult situation from which there was no point of return to normal. And it just felt plain weird. I had assumed that by the magical six-week mark my situation would have changed. All the books and all the midwives and anyone else who was lucky enough to have raised their children out of babyhood assured me earnestly that 'things got better' at around six weeks. Breastfeeding would be established, my baby would settle into a recognisable pattern of feeding and sleeping and I would have regained some energy after six concerted weeks of catnapping around the clock in sync with my baby's habit of sleeping in two-to-four-hour stretches throughout the day and night. My expectations were made unrealistically higher by all those other helpful parents who shook their heads in wonder at my self-confessed fatigue and confided that they wouldn't know what sleep deprivation felt like as their baby slept right through the night from the age of four weeks. To them all I sent a silent but violent raspberry.

At six weeks I was completely unable to make any sense of the days as they blurred on by. Getting up several times a night to feed Xena made me feel like I was starring in *Groundhog Day*. Yep, there she was — crying out for a feed again. Stagger up, feed from one breast, change her nappy, offer other breast, then lurch back to bed. And repeat, starting with the last breast offered in the last feed — but who the hell could remember which one that was, anyway?

On days when I managed to shower before lunch and visit the real world for a nanosecond, I found myself looking at other people in a new light. With envious eyes I watched people walking dogs, taking children to the park or sitting quietly over a cappuccino. Would I ever be able to do those things without having to lob out a breast, wipe a backside or calculate the approximate time I had left until the next feed? It didn't seem likely. At my worst I found myself wishing another baby on these people, just to shatter their peace. I didn't care if they had done their time and were reaping the rewards of surviving their children's babyhood; all I knew was that I was desperately jealous of the freedom they flaunted. I wanted that freedom, badly. I wanted to sleep. I wanted to go to the supermarket without feeling like I was on borrowed time. I wanted to wear clothes without buttons, wet patches over my breasts and vomit on my shoulder. I wanted to be the woman whose baby slept in a basket under the table at restaurants. If I couldn't have those things, I wanted a nanny—or, at the very least, a wet nurse.

Guiltily, I consoled myself with the thought that maternity leave was just that—a period of leave. I didn't have to be a stay-at-home mum forever. And then Xena would go and do something impossibly cute, like flap her arms and legs when she saw me unfasten my maternity bra, making me feel incredibly guilty for wanting to break away from such a helpless innocent.

🐤🐤🐤

If anyone needed a turning point, Xena and I did. Despite the promise of an established breastfeeding routine by six weeks, we were still struggling. Some feeds were good, but others were disastrous and left me wondering if she'd drunk anything at all. I felt lucky to escape the cracked and bleeding nipples, and recurring bouts of mastitis that other mums suffered, but I still had plenty of grief trying to make a silicone nipple function like a real one. I hated the stupid thing, but it was the only way Xena would feed.

It didn't help matters that I was off-my-nut tired. Every day felt like a week and every week felt like a month. A notebook in the loungeroom was covered with feed times and durations as I desperately tried to make sense of Xena's feeding and sleeping patterns and to unearth some sort of routine. What I actually discovered was that she had no routine whatsoever—and I had even less of an idea of how to change this (if indeed changing a six-week-old baby's behaviour was even possible; I suspected it was not). So my coded notebook scribbling grew in length: '1.15 am, 40 mins, left; 4 am, 30 mins, right; 7.30 am, someone please save me from this torture—now'.

I was tired because, despite the urgings of every single baby book known to womankind, I didn't sleep when Xena slept.

Five good reasons to sleep when your baby sleeps

New mums lose more than 200 hours of sleep in their baby's first year. This inevitable consequence of having a baby is known to affect your mood, emotions, concentration, health and ability to think rationally. It's not just a tired old parenting cliché: catching up on sleep really is far more important than doing housework. In fact, studies have revealed the following interesting facts:

- Mums who had less than five hours of sleep each day when their babies were six months old were more likely to retain baby weight than

I just couldn't; it felt wrong. If I had hopped in and out of bed when she did, I wouldn't have been able to shower, get dressed, eat meals, wash dishes and attend to the growing pile of puked-on bibs, Bonds jumpsuits, bassinette linen and chuck rugs. I wouldn't have felt like I'd had any life. Pathetic as it sounded, ducking my weary head under a shower and washing a few dishes helped me retain a vague sense of normality to my day—the key word here being 'vague'. Perhaps the real reason why sleeping during the day didn't work for me was that, far from settling into a better sleeping routine, Xena regressed in the sleeping stakes and big blocks of daytime sleep were no longer guaranteed. In her first few weeks, she had fed, fallen asleep and then

Take 10

A 10-minute nap (this effectively means lying down and closing your eyes for 10 minutes) has been identified by researchers as the most effective way to stay alert during the day. This should be doable even if your baby only catnaps. Alternatively, you could try lying down and closing your eyes for 10 minutes while breastfeeding.

mums who had at least seven hours of sleep per day.

- Lack of sleep and PND are related, with excessive fatigue and sleep disturbance considered early warning signs of PND.

- Most people can't function well on less than seven hours of sleep per day.

- Sleep isn't like a bank account where you can stock up for the future, or where you need to pay back what you have 'spent' —one good night's sleep will make up for several weeks of sleep deprivation.

- Broken nights really won't last forever, so submit to the necessity of a 5 pm bedtime for just a few weeks until your baby settles into more civilised sleeping and waking hours.

slept for up to three hours throughout the day. Now she would feed, stay awake for a confusing hour or so when I didn't know what to do with her, and then sleep for a grand total of forty minutes. When she woke crying and cranky, I was stumped. It was too early for another feed; she was too young to enjoy playing under a play gym; and she was basically too tired to be any fun at all. In desperation, I would usually plonk her in the pram and go for a walk around the block, which always seemed to settle her. But when we got

Helping your baby sleep

Teaching your baby good sleep habits is the first step towards you getting more sleep. You'll find a multitude of experts and books on the subject, but the important points to remember include the following:

- Establish an end-of-day bedtime (even if your baby is still waking for feeds throughout the night).

- Create a bedtime routine, such as bath, boob or bottle, swaddle and bed. These become familiar

back home and I tried to transfer her into the basinette, she'd wake and I'd be back at square one. As soothing as it was for her, I couldn't walk her around the block all day. I was tired from lack of sleep as it was, and a non-stop walking program would only deplete my energy levels further. The car was another alternative, but therein lay a similar problem: the car always lulled Xena back to sleep, but it had the same effect on me, which made the entire prospect downright dangerous.

Night-time was better in terms of the blocks of hours she slept between feeds, and some nights I got one good block of five hours' sleep, usually between the highly inappropriate times cues for your baby that it is time to sleep.

- Keep night-time feeds brief and functional, not playful and stimulating.

- Put your baby to bed drowsy but awake, so he or she learns to nod off and go back to sleep if woken during the night (much like we adults do).

- Make sure bub gets lots of fresh air during the day to improve the chances of good daytime naps. Often babies start sleeping for longer during the night after they start having regular good sleeps during the day.

of 5 pm and 10 pm, and then three- or four-hour blocks until 6 am or 7 am. If only I could have gone to bed for my main night's sleep at 5 pm, I might have started to feel a little better. But I just couldn't bring myself to do it, as this was the only time the Big Guy and I got to spend together without someone having to hold, feed, change or bath Xena. From 5 pm to about 7 pm we actually felt like a normal couple, cooking dinner and talking—about Xena, of course, because I was literally unable to contribute to any other topic of conversation. Then I'd grab a couple of hours sleep before the next feed.

Every night I put myself to bed, hoping, wishing and praying that by some miracle Xena would keep on sleeping through till morning. And every night at exactly 10 pm Xena informed me in her own special way that my dream hadn't come true by calling me from my inadequate slumber to fill her tiny belly. Sometimes the Big Guy was heading off to bed when I was getting up for that first night feed. I'd have hated him for that if he wasn't nice enough to sit up with me while we did what we had to do. Little did he know that while he sat there with his mutely feeding wife, I was wishing that he would suddenly grow breasts. Big, full, lactating breasts with enough milk to feed a small nation. Should this have happened, I would have happily handed over my baby and toddled off to sleep for the next three years.

Book in a doona day

If you feel dangerously sleep deprived (like you'd kill for a kip), ask your partner or a relative to look after your baby for the day while you disappear into your bedroom and under your doona, only surfacing for feeds when needed.

When even the nights started to go haywire and Xena began to wake more frequently than every three or four hours, I started questioning this whole parenting game. Babies should start sleeping for longer as they got older, or so I was led to believe. Six weeks into the game I now had a baby that had virtually no sleep during the day and woke even more frequently during the night. What on earth was going on?

I started fixating on formula as the magic key to settling Xena into a routine, torturing myself with unanswerable questions: Was she getting enough breast milk? Was she not sleeping because she was always hungry? Would she sleep better with a belly full of formula?

Our second visit to Doris at four weeks had revealed that Xena was putting on minute amounts of weight, but at least she wasn't losing weight. When I'd asked how to go about choosing between the different types of formula, Doris had urged me to 'keep it up for another two weeks'. By then I had hung around Doris for long enough to know that 'it' meant breastfeeding.

Demand feeding

Back when our parents had us, babies were fed every three or four hours and not before—no matter how much they screamed for an appetiser. Nowadays many experts, including advisory bodies such as the WHO and the Australian Breastfeeding Association, encourage demand feeding, especially if you're breastfeeding. This means feeding your baby whenever he or she demands it—around the clock. This can work really well for mums and babies who are prepared to 'go with the flow', so to speak.

But not everyone is a fan of baby-led feeding and some mums find the situation untenable, especially if their babies are demanding to be fed every hour around the clock and aren't sleeping well in between feeds. You will also find some babycare experts who still advocate strict feeding times. They believe this helps establish a good routine for babies and better sleeping habits. Personally, I see merit in both approaches, although strict feeding times may not work for newborns. It's up to each family to figure out which approach does or doesn't work for them.

The Big Guy didn't appear to struggle as much as I did since he'd gone back to work. I secretly suspected that he was as relieved to escape the confines of Compound Xena as I was resigned to a life of slavery. In some ways the Big Guy had found a degree of freedom again, so he could pick himself up off the floor after sharing two weeks of difficult days and shattered nights and re-immerse himself into life. He would wake up (once!) every morning, feed and dress himself without having to juggle a baby in the meantime, and then take his leave. I contemplated throwing myself at his legs every morning and begging him not to go, but usually chose not to out of fear of squashing Xena, who was normally hanging off my breast—encased as it still was in a plastic shield—at that particular time of day. I'm sure she latched on for dear life when she sensed her dad was about to leave. Smart kid. She probably knew I was sorely tempted to follow suit.

The contrast between our daytime responsibilities put the first stresses and strains on my relationship with the Big Guy. Conversation of the non-Xena variety was nonexistent. Physical contact was nil, which was a noticeable loss given our previously physical existence. The only time we touched was when we passed Xena, passed the baby wipes or passed each other like ships in the night in the bedroom. Even though I mourned the loss of our closeness, I was either busy feeding, changing or bathing Xena, or simply too tired to do anything about it.

Creating the right conditions for sleep

Not being able to get back to sleep after a night feed or resettling your baby is almost worse than having to get up in the first place. If you find yourself wide-eyed and staring at the ceiling long after your baby has been sent back to the land of the nod, the following tips might help:

- Limit your caffeine intake to no more than two cups of coffee or four cups of tea per day.

- Use blockout blinds to create a dark bedroom.

- Make your bedroom conducive to rest and sleep by removing computers, mobile phones and any other electronic or flashing distractions.

- Invest in the most comfortable bed linen and pillows you can afford.

- Use dim lighting when you need to get up in the night.

- Treat your bedroom like your sanctuary, not a dumping ground for everyone's junk.

- Ensure you spend some time outdoors every day. Exposure to bright outdoor light, especially in the morning, is said to help both you and your bub sleep more.

- Try to have one 30-minute walk per day, preferably in the earlier part of the day.

Chapter 10

Days *from hell*

One day I yelled at Xena. And I mean really yelled. I marched into her room, yanked her up from the cot and bellowed, 'For goodness sake, will you just bloody well sleep!' For a few seconds she stared up at me with wide frightened eyes. Then she started to howl. Not knowing what to do next I joined in, hugging her close to my chest, sobbing 'I'm sorry, I'm so sorry', over and over again. It was a wretched moment; one of those you really wish you could erase.

Xena was dead tired — she'd been awake for two hours — but she still refused to sleep. I fed her and put her into her cot, where she lay crying, getting more and more worked up by the minute. I went into the nursery at five-minute intervals, picked her up, patted her and then put her down again.

She cried. I rolled her on her side, reinstated her dummy and patted her bottom. She cried. I rocked the cot back and forth on its wheels. She cried. This went on for nearly an hour before I snapped. Perhaps I'd have been able to handle it had I not been up all night settling her every couple of hours but, as it was, I too was beyond exhaustion. Too tired to go for a calming walk, I did the next best thing: I went berko instead.

Fragile goods

I used to wonder who on earth would handle a baby roughly—until I had one, and discovered how frazzled and furiously tired mums can get. And how easy it is to snap. If you ever feel like you could shake, hit, throw or harm your baby, stop, place bub safely in his or her cot and call someone you trust for help.

Feeling sick with remorse, I rang the Big Guy to confess my sins and beg for forgiveness, but he didn't have the slightest clue why I felt the need to call. As far as *he* was concerned, there was no harm done and he couldn't understand why I was beating myself up about the incident. I was beginning to realise that we were no longer on the same wavelength since Xena's birth.

All up, that horrible day was a record low point in my life since Xena's birth. Yelling at her had felt good for the five seconds it took to get the frustration off my chest, but my guilt and remorse hung around like a bad smell all day, making me feel sick to my stomach. Unwittingly, I'd just initiated myself into a new stage of motherhood: welcome to the wonderful world of guilt, and have a nice day if you can scrape your morale up out of the gutter.

❧❧❧

Beyond tired: what to do with an over-tired baby who just won't sleep

Oops! So you've missed your baby's tired signs and now bub is frantic. It's time to throw all your rules out the window and do whatever it takes to get your baby to sleep. This includes (but is by no means limited to) the following sleep props:

- placing one hand on the left side of your baby's chest and using the other to pat his or her tummy in time with the heartbeat

- rocking bub in your arms or in a rocking chair

- bouncing on a fitness ball with your baby in your arms

- running a warm, relaxing bath (for baby, silly, not you!)

- feeding your baby—again!

- carrying bub around in a sling

- walking the baby around in the pram

- driving around in the car with your baby (just make sure you're not too tired to drive safely)

- placing a ticking clock or metronome in the baby's room (no bombs, please)

- playing some relaxing music (may I suggest any classical music compilation featuring the words 'most beautiful', 'soothing', 'romantic' or 'swoon' in the title)

- popping bub in a rocker and using your foot to bounce it up and down gently (while you collapse in a chair). A baby hammock, motorised swing or cot rocker does the swinging and swaying for you.

Remember, like a painful gallstone, this phase too will pass.

It was pointless bringing up the incident again with the Big Guy when he got home that night, because he really couldn't relate to my problem. The only problem he could see was that I had made a mountain out of a molehill. The yelling? Well, he said, all mothers yelled at their children. True, but to be fair I could have at least waited until she could yell back. I really needed to get the issue off my chest but wasn't sure who would help me off-load.

Coping with mother guilt

Every mum makes mistakes from time to time—any woman who says she doesn't is lying. The important thing is to learn from your errors, work out how to avoid doing the same thing again and then move on. Wallowing in guilt will only undermine your confidence and set you up to make more blunders.

I called a friend I hadn't spoken to in many months, singling her out because she had a two-year-old daughter whose arrival had coincided with the departure of the sparkle in my friend's eyes. Rumour had it that her child was a 'difficult baby' and I wondered if she could tell me whether mine was, too. This turned out to be a bad choice. My attempts to draw her into conversation about how hard it was to be a mum were met with a nervous laugh and a polite cliché, before the subject was changed. 'It gets better', she said. 'Have I told you that Molly says three-word sentences?'

More than ever I needed to talk, so I trawled through my phonebook, landing on the number of my cousin in Queensland, the mother of two boys aged six and four. We'd always been quite close but hadn't spoken for months and, although she wasn't really the type to indulge in deep-and-meaningful conversations about the philosophy of parenting, some instinct told me that she had the sympathetic ear I needed. So I called, and what perfect timing—my cousin had just opened a bottle of wine for her Friday night wind-down with her partner, and was primed for a chat.

We ran through the preliminaries of ages and stages of her kids, before the conversation came around to Xena and my eternal quest for sleep. I confessed I would quite happily have killed for a baby that slept during the day and all through the night. 'Here's a tip,' said my cousin, 'put a teaspoon of rice cereal in a bottle of formula to give her at night. It'll fill her belly and make her sleep longer.' I'd heard a variation of this tip, where crushed Milk Arrowroot biscuits replaced the rice cereal, but I didn't tell my cousin that. I also didn't tell her that her so-called 'tip' would horrify any health professional, given that they strongly advocated exclusive breastfeeding for the first six months and *absolutely no solid food before this time even if your child is starving, all right*? She may have caused horrendous damage to her boys by drugging them with formula and Farex, but far be it for me to spill the beans.

Dealing with other people's outdated advice

Parents who've been there and done that naturally want to share advice that worked for them. But when it comes to informing your aunt, cousin or mum that times have changed, it's important to be diplomatic. Their advice was perfectly acceptable back in their day, even if it's not now, and they don't deserve to be made to feel like a bad parent for following it.

Still, the talk was so therapeutic that I found myself promising to fly up for a 10-day visit, even though we didn't really have the money for a plane ticket and I hadn't bothered to run the plan by the Big Guy. Not once did I think about such practicalities as money or the logistics of travelling alone with a baby that I was struggling to look after in the comfort of my own home. I needed to go, and that was that. In many ways I wasn't surprised to find myself having committed to do something so out of the blue. Since having Xena I had found myself in some unnatural situations; this trip would just be one more unnatural situation in the scheme of things.

When I hung up the phone and sheepishly confessed to the Big Guy that Xena and I were going to abandon the homefront in the not-too-distant future, he backed me with unconditional support. 'Do what you need to do, spend what you need to spend', he said. He may not have been struggling with the day-to-day caring for Xena, but he was certainly struggling with the day-to-day caring for me, because I certainly wasn't the woman he'd married. He didn't say this out loud, but he didn't need to. Deep down I knew we'd already parted company.

Xena and I were due to fly out in six weeks.

Bad day pick-me-ups

We all need some coping strategies for really bad days. Here are some simple ways to take time out to regroup and face another day (or even just the rest of the day):

- Pop your baby in a pram and go somewhere that invigorates you. Ideas include an art gallery or museum, the botanic gardens or beach. Sometimes just getting out among other human beings or soaking up some gorgeous scenery is enough to pick you up, and your baby will most likely sleep through it all.

- Phone a friend (preferably one who's nearby and available for you to lob on over for the cry, laugh and Tim Tam fix you need).

- Declare a mattress day. Put your bed mattress

and pillows on the floor of the lounge room in front of the TV and snuggle up with your baby to watch chick flicks all day long. This day is all about gentle play and rest, in the one comfy location. No chores allowed.

- Beg a babysitting favour from a friend or relative. Then go and see a movie by yourself, in the middle of the day. It's a mere two-hour break that will make a world of difference to your ability to cope once you return to your motherly duties.

Chapter 11

Bottles, babysitters and *bedroom antics*

When the Big Guy cheerfully suggested to me that we spend some quality time together, I guessed it was his very polite way of asking 'Can we have sex again, please, if it's not too much bother?' Mistakenly, I had told him that I'd been declared fit for action at my six-week post-birth check-up and I think he interpreted that as meaning open slather in the boudoir again. Well, bugger it. I'd make him buy me dinner first and then decide whether or not I was ready, willing and able. Deep down, though, I knew the decision had already been made: I was happy to organise a babysitter and go out on a dinner date because, let's face it, a woman needs to eat, but there was no way I was putting out. If it came down to the crunch—sex or sleep—I would have quite cheerfully crossed my legs and dotted my 'i's on a contract for an uninterrupted night of rest.

The other thing bugging me was the whole babysitter thing. Who would mind Xena? And what if she woke for a feed while we were out? The answers, of course, were Mum (who I promptly rang to tee up a date) and a bottle (which I bought after an hour-long reconnaissance at the baby sections of every pharmacy and department store at my local shopping centre). Bewildered by the claims, features, endorsements and disparity of price, in the end I opted for an anti-colic variety, because even though Xena didn't have colic, I wanted to be *sure* she didn't have colic. It also had a unique airflow system, patented valve and silicone teat—her favourite flavour. About the only thing it didn't do was burp the baby. Naturally it was the most expensive one, too, which helped somewhat to assuage my fear: if I had bought the wrong type of bottle, at least it was a damn good wrong type of bottle.

Battle of the sex-less

It's important to acknowledge your partner's desire, even if you can't bring yourself to satisfy it. You could say, 'Darling, I know you're horny, but can we just have a cuddle tonight instead?' It may not be exactly what he had in mind, but it sure beats getting the cold shoulder and breeds much less resentment.

The trouble with colic

The condition known as colic has been the subject of a recent U-turn in parenting advice. Colic was previously thought to be a medical condition related to feeding techniques and wind, and characterised by excessive crying, irritability and general fussiness in young babies. A baby who cried for hours on end for no apparent reason, or was unable to be settled and had unpredictable sleeping patterns, was often described as 'colicky'. There was no known cure-all treatment for colic, and parents were

Purchase made, I set about trying to introduce this amazing contraption to Xena in the week leading up to the big event. Even though I pumped out milk at the end of every feed, it still took two days to get what looked like an adequate supply of expressed milk. Quite possibly I'd be faster next time but, as it was, progress was slow because I tipped over the first bottle with my overzealous pumping action and then I accidentally poured the second batch of expressed milk into the bottle before it had been sterilised. Hey, I was still on my L-plates. Finally, I had a decent offering in our whizz-bang, germ-free artificial bosom. After only two pathetic attempts to push away the teat with her tongue, Xena took to the bottle like a nipple-shield-fed baby to a silicone teat. Our romantic night out was looking good.

On the actual night of my dinner date with the Big Guy, Mum and Dad arrived, scooped up Xena from my arms, dismissed the A4 list of instructions I'd spent all day compiling and propelled us out the door. 'Have a good night, we'll be fine', Mum assured me. 'We *have* had our own children, you know.'

usually simply advised to batten down the hatches and endure this stage, which tended to peak at around six weeks and gradually decreased.

Nowadays, health experts are pretty adamant that there is no such thing as colic and that it certainly isn't a medical condition. They say that crying and fussing is a normal part of a baby's development that only gets better with time. And guess what? The advice hasn't changed, either—it's simply a case of doing what it takes to get you and your baby through this baffling phase. And on that note, it's unlikely that an anti-colic bottle is going to be of much help.

'Yes fine, Mum, but if nothing else, read points six to 15', I yelled back over my shoulder. 'It gives you a checklist to run through in case she won't settle after a feed. Oh, and there's seven bottles of breastmilk in the fridge—if she gets through that call me on the mobile...' The door slammed behind us and we were away.

The last time the Big Guy and I had sat in the car together, alone, was the night (or morning) we had headed off to hospital after my waters broke. I said as much to him, which made his face go all mushy. Chances are he was just about to say something really deep and meaningful, but I never found out what, because suddenly I shrieked, causing him to slam on the brakes. 'What's wrong?' His once mushy face was now etched with concern. 'I forgot to tell Mum not to microwave the breastmilk', I wailed tragically. 'You're not supposed to do that. What if she does it and Xena gets sick?' At the mention of a potential health risk to his little girl, the Big Guy quickly dialled home. Mum answered, in her 'will you just settle, petal' voice, which I ignored in favour of rescuing Xena from a fate worse than drinking from an anti-nothing, unpatented, el cheapo bottle. And then we were really on our way.

Still a good 10 minutes away from our destination, the Big Guy offered to drive home after our meal. Oh brother. Now I was 100 per cent certain he wanted sex and I wasn't sure how I was going to break the bad news to him. I decided to think about evasion tactics over a glass of bubbly with dinner, but once seated inside the cosy restaurant, I decided I couldn't wait that long, ordering a pre-dinner drink before I'd even glanced at the menu. The champagne felt so good as it made its way into my bloodstream that I quickly ordered a second to have with my meal. By the time we reached dessert I was feeling tipsy—hooray, I was a cheap drunk again!—and had forgotten that I was breastfeeding, so I had a third drink.

Bottle buying for dummies

You could be forgiven for thinking you need a degree in medicine to choose a baby bottle these days. The health claims and breastfeeding references plastered all over the packaging of the dozens of bottles available on the market can mislead you into thinking that your choice is much more important than it need be. Buying a bottle boils down to two things: your budget and your personal preferences. There are, however, a few things to bear in mind:

- Once you choose your brand of bottle, select the teats to match.

- Start with newborn flow and increase to match your baby's age or to keep up with his or her sucking pace. If bub starts gagging, the flow is probably too fast, but frustration at feeds is likely to be a sign that the flow is too slow.

- Some of the fancier bottles can be harder to clean—check how many parts are involved.

- There is some evidence that plastic bottles containing Bisphenol-A (BPA) may potentially cause health problems, although further research into this claim is needed. There are plastic BPA-free bottles available, but bear in mind some of the materials used to produce these bottles are untested, and not everyone in the industry is convinced BPA may cause harm.

- Glass is BPA-free and an environmentally friendly choice, but it also has a shatter factor if dropped.

- The squat, wide-mouthed bottles are generally thought to be easier to fill, with less spill factor than long, tall bottles with smaller openings.

- You'll need about six bottles (240 to 250 ml per bottle) each day for a fully bottle-fed baby.

Not surprisingly I soon needed to visit the rest room, where I promptly forgot that trouser zippers don't do themselves up. Oh no, the Big Guy had noticed my undone fly and thought I was coming on to him. 'You've got it all wrong', I felt like saying. 'I'm not being saucy and provocative, just drunk and disorderly. This is all about dinner—nothing more, nothing less.' In a pathetic attempt to distract him, I struck up a conversation about golf, which I quickly realised was an even bigger mistake than inadvertently flaunting my underwear. Now he would think I was wooing him by talking the language of his one great love (after myself and Xena, of course).

The final crunch came when the waiter appeared offering coffee. I knew it was all over red rover when the Big Guy smiled knowingly and announced we'd have coffee at home. Oh, this was just great. An undone zipper, a stupid error of judgement

Making love after giving birth

Regardless of whether you've had a caesarean or vaginal birth, it's a good idea to wait until your GP or obstetrician gives you the all clear at your six-week check-up before you and your partner get up close and intimate again. Your body needs this time to heal, internally and externally, especially if your baby was born by caesarean or you had stitches. Getting physical before you're ready can be painful and uncomfortable, and may even cause future problems—including feeling too scared to ever contemplate having sex again! Knowing you're physically ready for action will also help you gear up mentally, especially if you're feeling a little nervous about how it's going to feel down there (and if the parts still fit!). The important things to remember are:

and now I was going back to his place (oh, all right, *our* place) for 'coffee'. We may as well tear up the sleep contract here and now. And it was my own pathetic fault. Thanks to birth, breastfeeding and nearly two months of sleep deprivation I had turned into a hopeless three-drink drunk, incapable of fending off amorous overtures. I consoled myself with the thought that it had been such a long time between bonks that, if in the event I accidentally succumbed, the deed would be done faster than he could say 'bloody frangers!' Another glass of champers also helped to ease my mind.

We spent our last half-hour at the restaurant talking about when we first met, sucked face and decided we loved each other. By the time we left the restaurant, I was leaning happily on the Big Guy, cheeks flushed and eyes glazed. Yes sir-ee, four glasses of bubbly and I was almost his.

- take things slowly and gently
- keep some lubricant handy just in case, and especially if you're using condoms
- your breasts may leak if you are breastfeeding, so if that bothers either party wear a bra and breast pads or try to feed beforehand (sexy, I know!)
- talk to your doctor about contraception before you hop back in the saddle, so to speak, to ensure you've got everything covered. Breastfeeding is 98 per cent effective as contraception if your baby is under six months old and your periods haven't recommenced, but therein lies the catch. How can you be sure you haven't started ovulating again or that your first post-baby period isn't around the corner? If the thought of back-to-back babies sends shivers down your spine, opt for more reliable contraception.

Back home for our debriefing from Mum and Dad, we discovered that Xena hadn't even woken for a feed since we'd left, which was probably not surprising given that we'd been away for a grand total of two hours and 12 minutes. This time it was us herding them out the door, as the Big Guy and I were both desperate to get to bed, albeit for different reasons.

Slipping into bed (oh who am I kidding, I staggered) it became obvious that the Big Guy was angling for a debriefing of his own. My first thought was to play dead. Dead drunk or dead tired, I could have taken my pick. My second thought was slightly more adventurous; after all, it had been a while…

☙ ☙ ☙

Two hours later I woke to the harsh cries of Xena and the steady pounding of my first hangover since before I became pregnant. (Or, more truthfully, since I knew I was pregnant.) As my memory of the night that had passed, and realisation of why my head hurt, kicked in, I couldn't help grinning. Call me weird, but I relished this moment. It meant that life was starting to return to normal. Forgetting all about the unused breastmilk stored in the fridge and that my own milk was probably laced with champagne, I fed Xena. Strangely enough, she then slept through until dawn.

Booze and breastmilk

Most experts agree that alcohol does pass through a mother's bloodstream to her breastmilk and that a standard drink takes the average body approximately two hours to process, but this is where the consensus ends.

Some believe that occasional, small amounts of alcohol in breastmilk will not harm a breastfed baby; others say even a small amount of alcohol will place stress on a baby's immature liver; while still others say drinking a standard alcoholic drink is perfectly safe for a breastfed baby provided you do so after a feed, not before, and that you then refrain from breastfeeding until your body and milk is booze-free again. Confused? Me too.

The final word should go to the Australian health guidelines, which advise against drinking alcohol at all while breast-feeding, but only because there is no known or guaranteed safe limit for your baby. They suggest avoiding alcohol in the first month and, after this time, limiting your intake to two standard drinks per day. The guidelines also recommend expressing milk in advance if you choose to indulge in a tipple or two.

Chapter 12

Finding *formula*

By the end of our second month of parenthood, we had slid into a terrible routine of having absolutely no routine at all—which would have been fine if Xena had been happy, but she didn't really conform to the 'happy baby' stereotype. The smile that appeared at four weeks had gone into hiding, replaced by furrowed brows and a wailing mouth that denoted general crankiness. Her constant crying, grizzling and need to be held just about tipped me over the edge, and consequently I didn't really conform to the 'happy mum' stereotype either.

I had spent a frustrating week trying everything in the book to get Xena to exceed the 40-minute limit she had imposed on her daytime sleeps, figuring that if she could just have one good sleep more might follow. On the advice of Doris, I stopped swaddling Xena in a bunny rug before popping her in the cot, as struggling to get her arms free from their confines appeared to be distracting her from sleep. She woke after 40 minutes. On the advice of books, I played a badly tuned radio just outside her door so that she would be lulled to sleep by the 'white noise'. She still woke after 40 minutes. On my own hunch, I ditched the white noise and pinned a thick blanket over her window to block out every ray of light. Forty freaking minutes. And on one really bad day, I even tried the rice cereal tip in a bottle of expressed breastmilk. Not only did Xena wake after 40 minutes, but I started lying awake at night worrying that I had caused irreparable harm to my poor child.

Novice as I was, I knew that Xena had become hopelessly overtired. (She and I both!) What I didn't know was how to help her move past her over-tired state and into deep fulfilling sleep. All I could do was feed her every hour-and-a-half, a situation that couldn't go on for much longer, let alone forever, which was how it felt at the time.

In desperation I rang a parenting helpline and tearfully explained my problem. The counsellor was very kind. 'Feed your baby, wrap her snugly and put her to bed on her back while she's still awake', she advised gently. 'If she wakes after 40 minutes and can't settle herself, pick her up, re-wrap her and put her back to bed as before.' I explained that my early childhood nurse had told me not to wrap her anymore and waited for the counsellor to provide an alternative solution. It never came. 'This organisation advises all parents to use wrapping as a settling tool', was the reply. Well that organisation was no help to me, I decided, and hung up more frustrated than ever.

That's a wrap

Wrapping your baby in a blanket or muslin wrap before bedtime is thought to help make your baby feel safe, snug and sleepy, and prevent the innate newborn startle reflex from waking bub before adequate rest has been had. It's also considered to be a great sleep cue: bub soon learns that after being bundled up it's off to bed, which is where sleeping happens. Wrapping works perfectly well for some babies, but others aren't so compliant and end up spending a great deal of energy struggling to get their arms out of the binding and getting cranky and more wakeful in the process. If your baby wrestles the wrap, you could try:

- *wrapping bub in a cot sheet*. This is bigger than a standard wrap and therefore harder to get out of.
- *opt for a specialised wrap.* Check out baby stores for specially designed wrapping garments that are much more sophisticated than plain squares of cloth. These can feature zippers, fasteners and other clever designs to keep bub snug as he or she sleeps.

Then again, why push the wrapping issue if it's keeping both you and your baby up all day and night? You could always pop bub in a sleeping bag to promote feelings of cosiness and security, or try establishing another sleep cue such as singing a lullaby or patting bub's bottom gently in time with the heartbeat when you put him or her to bed.

The situation seemed hopeless and future prospects of Xena ever having a decent sleep looked bleak. How could she sleep when she was always feeding? And if she was always feeding, didn't that demonstrate that she was permanently hungry?

The only thing I hadn't tried loomed larger and larger in my mind, becoming an equally compelling and confronting thought: formula. 'Try it,' a voice whispered enticingly in one ear, 'it can't hurt her.' 'Don't even go there,' another voice countered strongly, 'you're doing the right thing by breastfeeding.'

The battle raged on in my head as Xena continued her war against sleep. Finally, after an emotion-charged showdown that ended in a semi-hysterical phone call to the Big Guy, I made my decision—and this time I wasn't going to be scared off by a stupid warning on a tin. Nothing else had worked to get Xena to sleep, but formula just might. I'd heard stories about formula-fed twins that had slept through the night from six weeks. My own mum told me that my siblings and I were formula fed from birth and had been hardly any bother at all. Perhaps it would perform miracles for us, too, so we headed off to the supermarket to begin the process of finding out.

How to choose infant formula

There's a simple reason why parents *don't* know where to start when it comes to buying formula: manufacturers and importers of infant formula follow a strict code of practice that prevents them from advertising their products directly to consumers. This is so they can't be accused of encouraging mums to give up breastfeeding in favour of formula. The facts you need to know are:

- Cows' milk formula is closest to human milk, so opt for one of those varieties first.

- Choose a formula designed for use from birth. Follow-on formulas are for babies older than six months, although you can also stick with a

Arriving at the baby aisle, I forced myself to view the range of formula products rationally, isolating all of the types that were suitable for Xena's age. When I'd identified my options, as per my bottle-buying rationale, I bought the most expensive one. If I was going to cop out, no-one was going to accuse me of taking the cheapskate option.

Xena was as excited as I was about her next feed, once she'd copped an eyeful of the bottle headed her way. Following our, ahem, dinner date, I had continued to give her the occasional bottle of breastmilk and I couldn't help but notice that, like me, she seemed to prefer these easy feeds. Perhaps she could sense my relief at not having to physically struggle through these feeds. Who knows? In any case, I'd been meticulous when making up that first bottle of formula, taking great care to heed the 79-step instructions that, unless followed precisely, may have caused my baby to self destruct. Well, that's pretty

'from birth' formula until 12 months if you like.

- Choose a brand that you can afford. The more expensive formulas have added nutrients, which are nice to have, but not absolutely necessary.

- Once you have made a choice, there's no need to swap over or try others. Having said that, if you can't find your particular brand one day and your baby happily takes a substitute, there's no harm in making that switch.

- Check with your GP before choosing soy or goats' milk or other specialised types of formula. True lactose intolerance — the common reason for avoiding cows' milk — is a condition that needs to be professionally diagnosed.

much what the tin said, anyway. Xena obviously had no complaints, and she certainly didn't self destruct. In fact, she didn't even question the bottle, let alone its unfamiliar-tasting milk, wolfing down every last drop without stopping for air. And then she opened her mouth and howled out for more. Given that I'd only made up the smallest amount, I made up that same amount again. And Xena drank pretty much the whole lot, again. This had to be so much more than the breastmilk she'd been getting from me. 'Please, please, please, let it have an effect on her sleeping', I prayed to the baby gods.

For the next few days I substituted the lunchtime breastfeed for a bottle of formula, but after the initial excitement caused by Xena's first one-and-a-half-hour sleep, she slid back into her usual ways. By then, however, I was sold on other benefits of hitting the bottle, and wasn't about to give it up. Formula gave me a delicious taste of freedom, allowing me to take Xena out during the day without worrying about doing the nipple-shield shuffle in public, or having to keep bottles of expressed breastmilk cool when not in use and warmed by non-microwave sources at feed time. Once confident that Xena's system was used to a daily bottle of formula, I decided to explore whether formula would have any effect on her night-time sleeping. I chose my target—the 10 pm feed—hoping against all hope that this would fill her belly so well that she'd sleep right past her usual 4 am feed, and maybe even through until real morning. (That would be any time starting with a six or a seven.)

But my hopes were very quickly dashed. After that first night feed of formula, Xena woke at 4.30 am, which, although marginally better than 4 am, was nowhere near the breakthrough I'd been foolish enough to expect. So now I was tired, frustrated and feeling guilty about reducing Xena's breastmilk rations to boot. Well, at least I was until the Big Guy offered to take over the 10 pm feed on a nightly basis. Oh happy days! This meant I could go to bed any time after Xena fed at about 6 pm, and enjoy eight or nine hours of uninterrupted sleep before the next feed at about 4 am.

The truth about sterilising

Most parents believe they need to sterilise their baby's bottles and teats for the first six or 12 months. The truth is that there is no research to suggest this prevents illness or infection—plus it's literally impossible to sterilise anything outside of a hospital environment because the moment a 'sterilised' bottle or teat is touched by human hands or even air, it's no longer sterile. Current advice recommends thoroughly cleaning bottles and teats before and after use, to get rid of any leftover milk residue and reduce the amount of bacteria present to a minimum. In simple terms, this means:

- washing new bottles in hot soapy water then air drying before use

- washing hands with soap and water when preparing bottles

- keeping kitchen bench tops clean and dry

- rinsing bottles after feeding

- using a bottle brush and hot soapy water to get milk residue out of nooks and crannies

- rinsing in hot water

- allowing to air dry, then storing bottles in a clean container.

However, if sterilising your baby's bottles, teats and dummies gives you peace of mind, go for it.

Formula-feeding frequency

While breastfeeding mums are encouraged to feed their babies 'on demand' and may not recognise a set pattern of feeding times, formula-feeding mums generally find that their babies tend to go for longer periods between feeds—plus they get into a habit of feeding at similar times each day. This is usually every three or four hours.

One reason for this is that formula tends to keep babies' tummies filled for longer. Breastmilk, on the other hand, is easier to digest and passes through bub's system faster. Another reason formula-fed babies feed less frequently is that the recommended daily amount of formula you need to give your baby (this is specified on the tin) has been calculated as the right amount to sustain a baby of that age for the day. So if you divide that amount evenly among bottles, and divide 24 hours by the number of bottles, and your bub drinks all or most of each bottle, there's no reason why he or she would need topping up before the next one is due. Of course, there are exceptions, but if your bub consistently drinks much more or much less than the recommended daily amount for his age, see your GP for advice.

As days went by I started to rely more and more on the bottles, be they filled with formula or expressed milk from feeds the formula had replaced. Either way, we had finished with the nipple shield, and by 10 weeks I pulled the plug on my breasts entirely, even abandoning the charade of expressing missed feeds to give by bottle later. There didn't seem much point continuing for the sake of saying 'Yes, I'm still breastfeeding my daughter'. Xena was feeding well and, after a flatulent couple of weeks while her system adjusted to the change in diet, made it clear that the amount of breastmilk I could express was hardly enough to keep her going. Formula on the other hand went the distance.

After their initial confusion, my breasts settled down. They even returned to their rightful position on my chest thanks to a supportive underwire bra. With barely concealed delight I threw the horrid shapeless maternity bras to the back of the cupboard, pegging a half-used box of breast pads after them.

Behold the change to my life: during the day Xena and I were free to get out of the house and during the night we all had more sleep. Even better, I could stop wearing button-down shirts. For us, switching to formula was a good decision that was further vindicated by our third visit to the health centre at 12 weeks. Finally, Xena had put on a decent amount of weight.

Hunger strikes

Your baby may want more or less formula than usual some days. Make up a little extra if bub drains the bottle and still appears hungry, but never force the issue if your baby leaves some formula. Just toss the dregs and offer him or her a freshly made bottle at the next feed, as it's unsafe to reheat and re-serve leftovers.

🦆🦆🦆

The Big Guy was jubilant that his daughter was finally gaining weight. Naturally I was as pleased as he was, but one thing still rankled me — the rice cereal I had slipped into Xena's bottle during that most desperate of desperate times when she just wouldn't sleep. I was really worried that I may have done some dreadful damage to her perfect little body by trying to drug her with food before she was ready. Reading through my library of baby bibles only increased my fear. They all recommended that solids be introduced between four and six months of age, because any earlier and Xena's system would be unable to digest the food effectively. Gulp.

But there was more bad news to come. Starting babies on solids earlier than the recommended age was also thought to trigger allergies and related conditions such as asthma. Oh no, I hyperventilated, what if she started having trouble breathing? For a couple of weeks I kept one hand on the zero button on the phone and two eyes glued to Xena as I watched vigilantly for symptoms of life-threatening Farex-induced conditions. Come the slightest gasp for breath or suspicious rash and I'd have had an ambulance at the door faster than you could say, 'It's all your fault, you rotten mother'. Fortunately nothing ever eventuated.

The closest we came to seeing an ambulance was a visit to my maternal grandmother, Xena's great-grandmother, at her retirement home. (From Nana's faithful accounts of which ailing golden oldies were checking in or out of hospital each week, I knew the local ambulance crew were regular visitors to the complex.)

'How lucky you are', said my Nana, looking proudly at Xena curled up in her arms. 'You have such a perfect life.

Thar she blows!

Beware the first fully formula poo—it's solid, smelly and just like a grown-up one! And it might take a little time to come out as your baby's digestive system adapts to the new diet, because formula is notoriously harder to digest than breastmilk. You'll probably notice the—ahem—frequent popping off at first. But if you see your baby straining excessively, going bright red in the face and generally struggling to get the little blighter out, or if you see pebbles instead of decent poos in the nappy, bub may be

Great husband, beautiful baby, nice home.' Just as I was beginning to think that I'd heard it all before, she said something that really caught my attention: 'It was much harder for us, you know.

'Just after your mother was born, in the middle of World War II,' she continued, 'our city was bombed. There was one other woman in the ward who had given birth at the same time as me and the doctors tried to get us to move into the bomb shelter with the other patients, but we refused to go. We held our babies tight and said, "No! We are not moving. We have just given birth"'. Nana went on to tell me how they stayed that way for the entire attack, just the two women and their babies, waiting for the bombs that may or may not claim their young lives.

While Nana and my then-infant mother had physically survived the bombing unharmed, six weeks later they faced another scary prospect when their entire family left everything behind and fled their war-torn country. As they travelled across borders, towards a safe haven, my six-week-old mother cried out for feeds that simply weren't available,

constipated. If this happens, see your GP or child health nurse for confirmation. They will most likely recommend one or more of the following things:

- checking you have followed the instructions on the tin exactly, including the correct scoop of powder-to-water ratio. Too much powder and not enough water can lead to constipation (but on the other hand, too little powder may not provide sufficient nourishment), so it's important to get the mix right

- giving your baby sips of cooled, boiled water in between feeds

- diluting prune juice with water to give to your baby.

as Nana had no breastmilk and certainly no formula to give. A kindly guard at one of the train stations between the many legs of the journey took pity on the young mum and her distressed baby, offering a cup of black coffee and a biscuit, which Nana mixed together to feed my mother. From then on my Nana fed my mother anything she could get her hands on.

Emergency feeding

If you happen to find yourself stranded with no formula and a hungry baby, a trusty GP assures me it's perfectly safe to feed your baby diluted cows' milk on occasions. For a six-week-old baby, add 30 ml of water to 120 ml of milk. For a three month old, add 30 ml of water to 210 ml of milk.

I hadn't heard either the story of the hospital bombing or the difficult trip across borders before, but I was certainly glad to hear them at that stage of my own journey. For starters, I now understood my mother's predilection to this day for strong coffee and continental biscuits. But, more importantly, Nana's story brought me crashing back down to earth with a jolting realisation that some mothers survived much greater challenges than I had ever or would ever face.

And there I was, fretting over a quarter teaspoon of rice cereal.

Chapter 13

From partners *to parents*

It had been three months since 'us two' became 'we three', but I was lonely. I missed the Big Guy. He hadn't really gone anywhere, mind you, but I missed him all the same. If anyone had gone AWOL, it was me—on a one-way trip to Planet Mum, hitching a ride on my very own shooting star. Had I been able to make a wish, I dare say I might have requested a ticket of leave occasionally, although I kept this secret to myself because the residents of Planet Mum seemed to be intensely loyal to this alien territory I had entered. Gentle probing of other inhabitants of Planet Mum was always met with an earnest declaration, complete with hand held over heart, that this was the best place in the world to live; that they couldn't remember what they did with their lives before taking residency. Not me.

I clearly remembered my former world, called Planet Me, on which I reserved the right to freedom of mind, body and soul. Planet Me was my turf and I reigned supreme. Sleeping in until midday and staying out until dawn were all mine for the taking. Watching movies, reading books, planting gardens and contemplating my navel were simple pleasures I took for granted. And the Big Guy, my much-loved mate of many years, was usually at my side making me laugh and feel good about myself.

We used to be a tight unit, the Big Guy and I, in sync both mentally and physically. Now, on a good day, one of us might remember to peck the other one's cheek in the afternoon when the Big Guy came home from work, but morning kisses had disappeared with Planet Me. It simply wasn't possible to kiss each other awake when one of us had been up several times in the night to feed or settle Xena while the other one was still catching up on sleep.

Baby-proofing your partnership

It's unrealistic to assume that your relationship will naturally cope with the changes a new baby brings without the investment of adequate time and energy to talk things through. No matter how rock solid you believe your partnership to be, and how well you know each other, the stresses and strains of caring for a new baby will most likely turn your cosy world on its axis, and sweeping all of these issues under the carpet will only create growing piles of resentment and discontent to deal with later on. Ideally, you should start discussing your changing roles and

Our new conversations revolved around settling techniques, lengths between feeds and nappy contents. Grocery lists and laundry duty also started generating some serious airtime. Much as I regretted their loss, deep and meaningful tete-a-tetes, kissing and cuddling were the furthest things from my mind. Xena now occupied my headspace, not to mention all of my available time, leaving no room for anyone else.

responsibilities when you start discussing which pram to buy and which shade to paint the nursery walls. If you overlooked that bit, it's never too late to discuss:

• your expectations about being a parent, including your values, beliefs and how involved you both want to be

• division of labour when you're both at home —including daytime and night-time duties

• time out for both partners, so no-one resents the other partner's freedom

• how to support both the breadwinner and the at-home parent so that neither feels as though they have the weight of the world on their shoulders.

Life on Planet Mum felt relentless to me. I thought that being a good citizen involved completely ignoring my needs in favour of my child's. Consequently I felt obligated to feed, settle, soothe and care for Xena at any given time on any given day, even when someone else—including the Big Guy—was around to do so. Every cry was attended, every snotty nose investigated, every waking hour spent feeding, changing or keeping my daughter company while she played under the playgym, kicked back in her rocker or attempted to introduce her fists to her tonsils. And just in case it wasn't enough to care for Xena around the clock, I also worried about how I was caring for her, striving above all else to Do The Right Thing, whatever that meant.

In contrast, the Big Guy seemed to adjust to parental status without having to change orbit. Granted, he looked a little more awkward than I did for the first few months when holding, feeding or changing Xena, but that was quite possibly because I was standing over him and telling him exactly how to do it. He sympathised with me over feeding problems and sleeping hassles, and did his best to help. But if he made a mistake or something didn't go to plan, he seemed to shrug it off, unable to understand why I worried over so-called 'little' things such as a missed sleep or a rejected bottle, or forgetting to pack a warm hat for Xena on a cold day.

Bring out your inner bloke

Let's face it, we women are known to overthink decisions and workshop countless 'what if?' scenarios. Try to get in the habit of adopting that wonderfully blokish 'she'll be right' attitude of not wasting time worrying before there's a genuine need.

Then again, he didn't seem to get the big things either. In particular, he didn't do guilt as well and as often as I did, reinforcing my suspicion that guilt was a prerequisite for admission to Planet Mum but optional on Planet Dad. There was no point berating myself for giving up breastfeeding, he said, because it was the best choice for us. 'Xena is healthy, putting on weight and even sleeping better', he reminded me. And had I forgotten that putting Xena on the bottle also freed me from being the sole feeder? Formula was a solution, not a problem, he said. The Big Guy didn't give a toss that I'd gone against every health professional's advice, but I worried about it, especially after I unwittingly exposed

Xena to an emerging case of chickenpox just one week after I had replaced her last breastfeed with a bottle.

When the news came through that my sister had been diagnosed with the worst case of chickenpox her doctor had ever seen, only hours after she'd cuddled up to Xena, I was as consumed by guilt as I was with worry. If only Xena was still being breastfed, I remonstrated, she would have had immunity courtesy of me. While I steeled myself for an outbreak of spots, the Big Guy wasn't the least bit perturbed: 'If she gets chickenpox, she gets chicken-pox', was all he said in response to my hair pulling and hand wringing. 'Most kids do, you know. I wouldn't worry about it.'

He'd nailed it in one: he wouldn't worry about it but I would, because not only was I the one who would have to look after our chickenpox-ridden child, but I was also the one who may have been able to prevent the illness in the first place. That the illness never eventuated gave me little comfort.

The difference between dads and mums was one of the few topics other mums and I agreed on wholeheartedly, often working its way into our conversations. The subject was always introduced in the same way: 'He's such a great dad, but ...' Among the usual bugbears were getting up to attend to the baby at night or in the morning, domestics and nappies. Fortunately for me, I didn't have a husband who balked at a pooey—but others did. I found it easy enough to chuckle at Mick, Sue's partner, who refused to change his son's nappy because it made him feel sick. But I couldn't find any humour in stories of leaking nappies at night, because failing to fasten nappies securely was a crime the Big Guy committed in the early days, and I was the one who copped the sentence of extra night visits to the nursery when wet bedding woke my sleeping baby.

Aside from night-time nappy debacles, I could laugh off most of these stories, but they brought me no closer to understanding the changes in my own relationship. And then the Big Guy's best mate, Fletch, helped set me straight.

Leak-proof nappies

As your baby gets older, sometimes a nappy might become so full at night that it leaks and wakes bub up. To prevent this, put your baby in a nappy that's one size bigger than the one worn during the day. Alternatively, try popping a maxi pad in the nappy for extra absorbency.

We were at a friend's place for a barbecue and, as usual, the men were beating their chests around the hotplate while we womenfolk congregated in the shade flanked by prams, nursing babies or chasing after tearaway toddlers. Our conversations — usually about the children — would start, only to trail off mid-anecdote when the relevant mum rushed away to rescue a dropped dummy,

Equal opportunity for dads

It takes two to make a baby, and it sure helps having two to raise one. The classic mistake many mums make is thinking that because they are the primary carers, they have to do everything themselves. We're lucky that this generation of dads want and expect to be actively involved in raising their children — it would be to all of our detriments if we curbed their enthusiasm by unwittingly channelling mother superior. Remember the following tips when sharing the load with your partner:

- Avoid being a helicopter parent who hovers over the co-parent, directing them on all matters baby.

untrap the odd head stuck between the legs of a chair or soothe a scraped knee. Once a story was interrupted this way, it was lost in the ether. No-one bothered going back to the cut-off point because we all knew that we'd never get to the end anyway, unless the story could be said in about four words before the next kid-related rescue mission. In contrast, each and every father in the group remained glued to their side of the barbecue, unless it happened to be their turn to get beers.

After a while I tired of all the baby talk and left the 'gatherers' of the group and wandered over to the 'hunters' at the hotplate to catch up with Fletch, the Big Guy's childhood mate and father of a little girl, Ruby, who was nine months older than Xena. He slung an arm over my shoulder and made a crack about the mothers' group scenario I'd just come from. I refrained from saying what I really felt—that the guys should have been sharing the childminding that had preoccupied the girls for the entire afternoon—choosing

- Allow your partner to learn babycare techniques through trial and error, just as you have done.
- Bite your tongue if your partner's way of bathing, changing, settling or feeding your baby is not exactly how you would do things. Your baby will happily adapt to both of you.
- Don't correct your partner's attempts to help you with the baby, or check up on every move. This only doubles your workload and makes your partner feel as though you don't trust him to be a good enough parent.
- Remind him what a great dad he is from time to time.

instead to make a fairly banal comment about it being a great day. I was actually referring to the weather, but Fletch interpreted the comment in another way altogether.

'Yeah, mate, I'm having a ripper', he agreed, kicking back and casting a proud glance towards the apple of his eye, who, as usual, was under the watchful eye of Fletch's wife, Sarah. 'This is what life's all about, isn't it?' With a couple of beers under my belt, my tongue was loose enough to beg to differ and I decided to let fly. 'No, Fletch, sometimes being a mum isn't the ideal life. I find it draining, exhausting, sometimes boring and often frustrating. Being a parent is the most difficult thing I have ever done, and everything I used to do without thinking—even coming here today—requires such an enormous effort that I am exhausted before I have even begun.' Couldn't he see what I was talking about? Couldn't he understand that sometimes I felt that being a parent was a trap, not a treat? No, he couldn't.

Shaking his head, and possibly saying silent thanks that his wife was the happiest resident on Planet Mum, he gave it to me straight. Being at home with a baby was beyond his comprehension. He had no idea what that involved and never would. 'Mate, you're talking to the wrong person here', he said kindly. 'My life hasn't really changed. I still get up in the morning and go to work. The only difference is that now there's one more person to come home to, and seeing her is the highlight of my day.'

He was right, of course. For the blokes, life *did* go on. They went to work, came home and saw the family as a lovely treat at the end of a hard day, whereas for women, the family *was* the hard day, and knock-off time was not written into the contract.

Chapter 14

Getting *away from it all—* with baby

Xena was just four months old when we found ourselves hurtling down the freeway towards the domestic terminal at the airport, destination Cairns.

Earlier that morning I'd had second thoughts about the trip, seriously contemplating calling the whole expedition off. Leaving the comfort of my home didn't seem like such a great idea in the cold light of the depature day. What if it all went horribly wrong and Xena was even more unsettled than ever? Would I have everything I needed to cope? More importantly, would it all fit in one suitcase and one piece of hand luggage?

Packing had been an absolute nightmare, made worse by the fact that we would be swapping winter for the tropics. We hadn't lived through a summer with Xena yet, so I had no idea how to dress a baby for the heat. In the end I packed her entire wardrobe, plus a few extra summer outfits I'd recently picked up especially for the trip. The little shortie rompers looked hopelessly inadequate and almost didn't make it into our bag. We'd been living with around-the-clock heating for the past two icy-cold months, and it seemed highly unlikely that I would ever feel confident that Xena was not going to freeze to death unless she was covered from head to toe in polar fleece.

Then there was all the feeding paraphernalia to drag across the border: bottles; bottle brushes; unopened tin of formula (in case I couldn't buy her specific type) and antibacterial tablets (as much as I had wanted to take the steam steriliser, there was absolutely no way I could find space for that big unit); a packet of rice cereal for our planned introduction of solids while we were away; and, finally, dummies, a few toys and, oh yes, an outfit or two for me. The travel cot, pram and rocker were all being hired by my cousin, so that took a small load off my mind. I'd crossed my fingers she hadn't forgotten to organise these essentials, and made the Big Guy sit on the suitcase while I forced its zipper closed. Taking a deep breath, I shut the front door behind us. Ready or not, here we came.

The Big Guy had insisted on driving us to the airport under the guise of helping with the luggage, which he didn't think I could manage while also lugging Xena. Having already become adept at managing seven full grocery bags in one hand, collecting the mail and opening the front door with the other while also carrying Xena in a pouch, I would normally have begged to differ, but chose to shut my mouth. Conscious of how crabby I'd been during the last few months, I guessed he probably wanted to make sure we actually left town. The poor bugger was as much in need of a break—from me—as I was.

In the end I was very glad for his escort. Xena had expressed her disgust at the long check-in queue by filling her nappy, so she and I left the Big Guy with our luggage while we headed off to the nearest parents' room, which was airport speak for a tiny overheated cupboard with a bench, sink and toilet. We'd just made it back to him when I discovered Xena hadn't quite finished her business, thanks all the same. So it was back to the changing room for the second time in as many minutes. By the time I reached the last press stud on Xena's jumpsuit we were both hot and bothered, and Xena had started crying. The Big Guy and I could do little more than pass our distressed daughter back and forth in those last few minutes before departure and I wondered again if I was insane for leaving home to do this somewhere else. Against the backdrop of Xena's wailing and our first boarding call, the Big Guy and I exchanged a quick kiss and worried looks. 'You'll be right', he said unconvincingly as I carried my screaming bundle through the departure gate. 'Have a great time.' Resolutely I walked onto the aircraft, patting, hushing and crooning in Xena's ear, but the only thing that was settled was the trip. Once on board, there was no turning back.

We landed at Cairns airport in a great mood, Xena bouncing up and down on her chubby little legs and grinning at the passengers behind us while I supported her standing on my lap. To my unexpected delight, the flight had been an absolute pleasure. I'd given Xena a nice warm bottle of formula upon take-off because I'd read that the sucking motion would ease any discomfort to her ears caused by the cabin pressure.

The bottle, combined with the drone of the plane, made her so comfortable that she fell into a deep sleep in my arms. Propped up with pillows brought to me by the attendants, I also dozed for the entire journey, occasionally peeling open an eye to check that Xena was still asleep. But all was quiet on that front: Xena had snuggled up onto my chest with her head so close to mine that I could feel her gentle breath on my neck. Her slightly furrowed brow and opened mouth gave the impression she was concentrating hard on the task at hand. Funny little thing. She could drive me crazy one minute and bring tears of joy to my eyes the next.

I couldn't tell who benefited most from that restful journey, me or Xena. Even before we had disembarked I felt more relaxed than I had in ages and started to think that perhaps this trip wasn't such a foolish idea after all.

Happy travels

Sure, you need a lot of stuff when you take your baby on holiday, but try to resist the urge to pack the kitchen sink and think about whether you can improvise what you need. You should probably consider hiring some of the following things when you travel with your baby:

- *cot.* Check if the cot you intend to hire comes with linen or if you need to bring your own.

- *car seat.* If you've travelled by plane but intend to hire or use a car, remember to hire a car seat, too.

- *high chair.* Using your stroller as a highchair

isn't ideal as food tends to get smeared and stuck everywhere.

There are also a number of things that you might be tempted to bring, but should consider leaving at home. These include:

- *baby bath*. If there's no actual bath, use a sink to bathe your baby or get bub used to being held under a shower.

- *toys*. Improvise with safe household items or buy a cheap set of blocks or similar for bub to play with and then leave behind.

- *too many clothes*. Keep tabs on the weather leading up to your holiday, and take a few appropriate-weight onesies that wash and wear.

There are some items that you will need to pack, because they are necessary and can't be hired. These include:

- *comforters*. Your baby may need some things to help getting off to sleep such as a dummy or wrap.

- *formula*. You can switch to another similar type of formula if you run out or can't find your particular brand at your travel destination, but you may get extra piece of mind bringing your preferred brand.

- *supplies for the journey*. It's important to bring enough bottles, nappies, wipes and food to last for your baby until you arrive at your destination and are able to stock up on more.

The first thing that struck me when we reached my cousin's place was that 'tropical climate' really meant tropical climate. Those fleecy jumpsuits and cardigans I had packed for Xena would just have to stay packed. The short rompers, on the other hand, were a great call and we'd probably need more of the same. Nothing that a trip to the shops wouldn't fix, I thought, rather cheered by the prospect of a spot of retail therapy. I was on holiday, after all, and had nothing more to do

Double check the details

If you have pre-booked baby equipment at your new destination to make travelling with your bub easier (perhaps a bassinette on the plane, baby equipment at your accommodation or a place at kids club or crèche), ring and confirm these details before you leave home rather than risk finding a stuff-up on arrival.

than relax and enjoy myself: there was no washing to be done, no housework to complete, no pressures on my time. Then and there I made up my mind not to stress over Xena, but to sit back and go with the flow for once. If Xena wouldn't sleep during the day, so be it. If she woke at night, I'd give her a bottle and do whatever else it took to get her back to sleep. Even the fact that my cousin forgot to hire a cot for Xena didn't faze me. No problem, I'd simply put her in the spare double bed with me.

In fact, sharing a bed turned out to be the best thing we could have done. Who knows if it was the sound of my breathing

Bunking in with baby

The question of whether it is advisable to share your bed with baby (also known as co-sleeping) provokes wildly divergent answers. Champions of co-sleeping say it promotes a feeling of security in your baby, closer bonding and easier breastfeeding. Other parents find it unnatural, uncomfortable (especially with babies who sleep in star-fish mode) and disruptive of a good night's sleep. On a safety level, the Australian authority on safe sleeping, SIDS and Kids, does not recommend that parents share an adult bed with their baby as there are too many potential hazards, including suffocation and entrapment. They do, however, suggest safety guidelines for parents to follow, should they choose to co-sleep. The key points to remember include the following:

• Place your baby on top of adult bedding, not

beside her or the mild nights that agreed with Xena, but on that first night she went to bed at 7 pm and slept soundly for 12 hours straight—a pattern that continued throughout our stay. Waking up in the morning to the sound of my little girl waking was a glorious way to start the day and infinitely preferable to the sleep-shattering crying I'd been used to. I'd watch her roll over onto her tummy, fix her big wide eyes on me in disbelief, and then see her face light up when she registered it was me, her mum. She'd smile, I'd beam and we'd enjoy a happy cuddle before we got up. 'Good morning' never rang so true.

I also discovered something I had suspected all along: once Xena's night-time sleeping was sorted, her daytime sleeping followed suit. By day two of our stay, Xena had settled into a habit of sleeping for two hours in the morning and two hours in the afternoon. Finally we had a recognisable

underneath, so bub can't slip under adult bedding or pillows.

- Ensure that your baby can't fall out of bed or become trapped between the wall and the mattress.

- Never co-sleep if you have taken medicine, drugs or alcohol that could cause you to sleep heavily (and potentially roll over and smother your baby).

- Always follow safe sleeping guidelines, including putting babies to bed on their backs, leaving their faces uncovered, ensuring they're warm but not over-dressed and keeping them away from cigarette smoke at all times.

A great alternative to actual bed sharing is placing your baby's cot by your side of the bed, with the cot's side lowered down. This allows you and your baby to sleep side-by-side, but in your own space. It also means you can reach bub easily for night feeds, replacing the dummy or patting back to sleep.

routine that was infinitely more workable than the old one (or lack thereof). There was no carrying on when I put Xena down for her naps, there was no 40-minute cat-napping during the day, and there was no night waking. There was just a delightful little girl who had finally realised that sleep was a good thing that made babies and their mummies very happy. Possibly the introduction of solids, which she had happily accepted, also helped put some structure into our day. I really enjoyed the early encounters between Xena's gummy gob and a spoonful of slop—or baby rice cereal, as it was. It always gave me the giggles to see her eyes double in size and her fists clench and shake in anticipation of this tiniest of meals. And I could hardly wait to see her reaction to an offering that didn't look (or smell) like baby sick! But, first things first, and so we continued with the ghastly (to me) rice cereal, all the while looking forward to the day not far ahead when I could start pureeing pears and pumpkin and other gastronomic goodies for my growing girl.

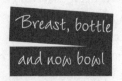

Breast, bottle and now bowl

Don't expect your baby to miraculously eat great quantities once you start feeding him or her real food. The first few weeks of starting solids is not about filling bub's belly. It's about practising taking and swallowing (not pushing out with his or her tongue) tiny amounts of food from a spoon.

With Xena settled into her new, wonderfully civilised routine, my cousin and I could concentrate on a little bonding of our own. My guaranteed night's sleep meant I could finally let go of my inhibitions enough to get back into a night life, albeit a much different variety of nightlife than I had enjoyed before Xena. With three kids between us we were homebound, but this didn't stop us from creating our own party each night.

Every morning we'd plan our menu, name our poison for the evening and look forward to the time when the little people were tucked away in bed and we could get on with the business of being us. 'Us', more often than not, involved a bottle of plonk, some old Linda Ronstadt albums played at full bore and a whole lot of try-hard singing.

When to start solids

Identifying the right age to start your baby on solid food can feel like a bit of a puzzle, especially when mums from different generations all offer differing opinions, which generally range from six weeks to six months. It's best to go with current Australian advice, which recommends not introducing solids before four months (as a baby's digestive system is too immature to handle anything other than breastmilk or formula before this age) and no later than six months (when the iron stores your baby is born with start to run out and need replenishing). Still, this advice is far from definitive and requires some decision-making on your part. If your baby is within the four-to-six-month age range and showing some of the typical signs of being ready to try something other than breastmilk or formula, consider it time to get out the plastic bowls and spoons. Typical signs of being ready for solids include:

- gnawing on fists, toys or anything within reach

- no longer seeming satisfied and settled after a milk feed

- being able to sit propped up

- holding up his head steadily

- showing clear interest in adult eating, if not notably drooling or imitating adults when they eat.

Daytime was spent sitting in the warm shade, watching my cousin's boys yahooing around their home. Xena seemed mesmerised by the older children, and would strain to catch sight of them climbing trees, playing in the sandpit or bouncing on the trampoline. The trampoline in particular tickled her fancy, and she would happily sit on my lap watching the boys rocket up into the sky, flip themselves over and land on their rascally little bottoms. It was during one of these cousin-watching sessions that it happened: the strange sound made its way up from deep within Xena, tumbling out of her mouth and lighting up her whole face. Her first laugh — the most beautiful sound I had ever heard.

Xena laughed several more times on our holiday, and I laughed more than I had in the last four months. I laughed at my cousin's boys, who asked all sorts of funny questions and made me realise that, as unlikely as it seemed at times, one day Xena would reach that age, too. I laughed as my girl explored her new surroundings by rolling into action — having left Xena on her tummy in the lounge room, I found her a few moments later hidden under the lounge, exploring the springs. I laughed during the amateur karaoke sessions, when my cousin and I had trouble reaching Linda's high notes but still gave it a good shot.

All up it was a blissful sojourn, and I was undeniably grateful to both Xena and my cousin for helping me rediscover how to enjoy, as opposed to endure, life.

It had taken four challenging months and a 2700-kilometre flight, but the journey had been worth it. Somehow or other, Xena and I had found our groove.

What goes in must come out

The introduction of solid food to your baby's diet can have an impact on what turns up in nappies and, if you're not in the know, some of the—er—*findings* may seem a little freakish, if not downright worrying. Bear in mind that little digestive systems take time to get used to new foods, which means you may see bits and pieces of those new foods until bub's system adjusts. Here are some common sightings that are harmless despite looking pretty horrid:

- black worm-like threads, usually from bananas
- purple or red poo from eating blueberries, beetroot or rhubarb
- orange-tinted poo from a diet of pumpkin, sweet potato or carrot
- very small black seeds can probably be traced back to kiwifruit or grainy bread
- whole peas, corn kernels and grains will start appearing when bub moves on from smooth blended foods to coarser textures.

Chapter 15

Choosing
child care

Once safely back home from our happy holiday in Queensland, a niggling thought that had been at the back of my mind worked its way to the front. My return-to-work deadline was looming and, aside from the obligatory 'check out my baby' visit to the office, I hadn't had much contact with my colleagues in the five months since having Xena. Tentatively I broached the subject with the Big Guy. 'Don't go back if you don't want to', he had offered gallantly. 'We'll get by.'

'Are you out of your mind?' I asked incredulously. 'Give up my last link with the life I once had?' Oh no, I was going back, and that was that. I loved Xena madly, but I needed to reclaim a fraction of my own headspace. Being at home with her had been an around-the-clock, seven-days-a-week job for months on end. It was time to expand my horizons or else risk completely losing sight of Planet Me. Besides, living on one income was not so easy after having been used to living on two for so many years, especially now that we were also continually incurring new costs. Our utility bills had grown in direct correlation to the number of days Xena and I had spent at home, with heating-related costs in winter soaring to dizzy new three-figure heights starting with the number four. Nappies alone set us back another $40 each week. Add a tin of formula, some baby food and all of our new 'must haves'—including a just-in-case-of-emergency stockpile of Xena's favourite dummies, rusks and gourmet baby food—and we may as well have transferred the Big Guy's salary straight to the supermarket cash register. And that was just for the ordinary day-to-day requirements!

Other options

A small lifestyle change might be the difference it takes to keep you at home for longer, if that's what you'd like to do. Think about whether you could downsize to one car or a smaller home, or reduce your regular outgoings in a way that makes you better off financially.

Then there were the one-off costs of setting up our baby, and every month and every season change would warrant another major outlay. We'd need a cot for when she outgrew her bassinette. Cotton sheets and light blankets for the warmer months ahead. Flannelette sheets, fleecy sleep suits and warmer blankets for the icy winter we were currently shivering through. A fan for summer. A heater for winter. A complete new wardrobe every few months because Xena was starting to change her dress size every time I blinked! A rocker for when she couldn't sit up unaided, a highchair for when she started solids, a car seat for when she would outgrow the hired baby capsule, a lightweight stroller for when we would finally get sick of carting around our bulky pram. Quite possibly we were still paying our mortgage, too, although I honestly couldn't see how we had any money left over at the end of each fortnight to do so. The list of needs went on, the bank balance went down and for the first time in our lives the credit card was maxed out. Aside from my own personal needs, there was no denying the more mercenary reason behind my decision to pick up my keyboard where I had left off: the time had come for Mummy to earn some money, honey.

The thought of combining my new life with my old one was more than mildly terrifying. Xena was sleeping through the night as a general rule, but every now and then she'd have a shocker and I'd be up every hour or two, finding and fitting her dummy, or bending over the cot bars to pat her back to sleep before creeping back to my bed, where the Big Guy was dead to the world, oblivious to what was going on in the next room. At other times she might wake up at 4.30 am or 5 am, and I'd give her a quick bottle before putting her back down in her cot for another hour or two. I couldn't imagine how I would manage to cope with broken nights and crack-of-dawn

Calling all parents . . .

Parental leave isn't just for mums. If you and your partner have both clocked up 12 months' continuous employment with your current employers, you can share between you a total period of 12 months' unpaid leave. You can't both be on leave at the same time, but if you take six months of maternity leave, he has six months of paternity leave to claim —if he's man enough!

mornings and still front up to the office to function in an even remotely responsible manner, but at the very least I would give it a try. So that I wouldn't chicken out, I rang my boss and confirmed the date of my first day. The next step was to organise some form of care for Xena, although I was secretly hoping someone kind would put up their hand and say, 'Here, let me look after your darling daughter', or that there would be a massive rationalisation of the nanny industry, making hiring a nanny an affordable option for the non-squillionaires among us. But that didn't happen so I rang the council instead, asking for a list of childcare centres in my area. Armed with the list, I made a few phone calls and started making my rounds.

Not exactly sure what I would find, but half expecting to see hordes of unhappy and abandoned children peering plaintively from behind great big scary fences, I was more than a little relieved to discover that both the children and the staff at day care looked normal. Not at all like the pitiful

Finding the right child care

Unless you are blessed with a trusted friend or relative who generously offers to care for your baby when you return to work, you essentially have three options when deciding what to do about child care:

- *long day care.* Centre-based child care on a full-time or part-time basis for working parents. Centres may be run privately or by local councils, community groups, employers and not-for-profit organisations. Daily fees per child will vary, depending on the operator and where you live. Licensed day care centres have a mix of qualified and unqualified staff and must conform to strict child-to-staff ratios and accreditation standards. For a list of centres near you contact your local council, visit the National Child Care Accreditation Council at <www.ncac.gov.au> or call 1300 136 554.

orphans and cruel wardens I had expected, which was a good start. In fact the kids looked like they were having tons of fun, tearing around outdoors or engrossed in activities indoors. Only once when I caught sight of a baby, alone, but busily playing with some playdough stuck on the floor, did I feel a pang. Oh Xena, could I really leave you alone like this with strangers?

Emotional confidence crises aside, the centres Xena and I toured looked great—and by the time I walked out of the third one, I was able to ask appropriately probing questions about babies-to-staff ratios, teaching qualifications, individual routines versus centre routines, catering facilities and whether or not nappies and/or formula were provided. I was also able to look into the nurseries without hyperventilating at the thought of my baby sleeping in a row of cots. I was shocked to realise that, if Xena was to attend day care,

- *family day care*. Child care for a small number of children in the carer's home (not yours) during standard business hours, as well as overnight, weekends, school holidays and before or after school. Carers are often mums who have been recruited, trained and monitored by Family Day Care Australia. To find a carer visit <www.familydaycare.com.au> or call 1800 621 218.

- *nanny*. One-on one child care in your home that is provided according to your specific needs, at an hourly or daily rate that is more expensive than group care. The nanny industry is not regulated, so you or the agency you employ to source a nanny should check the identity, references, qualifications and 'working with children' status of your chosen nanny. You can find a nanny through an agency specialising in home help, via the internet or through word of mouth.

she would have to sleep like this. It had taken months to get her sleeping soundly through the day—would all that hard work be undone once she discovered she would soon be expected to sleep in baby prison, along with the other inmates? Would she put up a fight again, and revert back to those horrid days when sleep was a battle, never to be won by me? Oh well, at least that wouldn't be *my* daytime problem, I acknowledged to myself (somewhat guiltily). Let them figure it out.

Finding good child care

Not sure what to look for when embarking on your search for early child care? Or how to compare different providers offering the same service? For a list of things to ask, check and consider when interviewing potential long day care centres and family day carers, visit <http://www.ncac.gov.au/families/families_choosingChildcare.asp>

There was only one problem with child care that I could see, and that was we might not be able to secure a place for Xena until she was almost old enough to leave home. Every single centre had an enormous and un-jumpable waiting list—some as long as 60 names—of babies wanting places in their centres. And each centre only took 10 babies! Apparently I should have organised Xena's care much earlier. Like upon the exact moment of conception. There was nothing to do but try my luck, so, like the hundreds of parents who had obviously got in way before me, I added my name to three waiting lists, tried hard not to choke when I learnt the daily rate, crossed my fingers and hoped against hope that we would secure a place within the next few months.

All about Grandcare

Grandma or Grandpa may seem like the dream child care choice, but think carefully before you go down this road, and make sure you nut out all the terms and conditions with your mum, dad or in-laws just as you would with a potential nanny or child care provider. You'll need to consider:

- *payment*. Free child care may come at another price, namely resentment and strained relationships. The child care provider may feel used and abused and you may feel unable to voice your opinions or raise issues with someone who is providing such a valuable service to you for zip. Sometimes negotiating a reasonable fee makes the arrangement run smoother.

- *views on child raising*. Have the conversation about the big issues before you seal the deal, not after you discover you and Grandma's views on smacking are worlds apart. Bear in mind you may both have to give and take a little to make this work.

- *location*. If they don't come to your home, you'll need to ensure theirs is baby-safe.

- *age and energy levels*. Is the potential arrangement realistic, given the health and ability of your carers?

- *holidays and sick days*. Your carers will need planned and unplanned time off throughout the year to have a break from the job or when illness strikes. Talk about holidays before they become a necessity, and have a back-up plan for when your carers get sick.

One month later we still didn't have a place guaranteed, but I felt quietly confident that something would come through at the right time. Childcare centres were for working parents, and that's what I was about to become — if they couldn't cater for me, who *could* they cater for? I put my trust in blind faith and sat back to enjoy my remaining few months at home with my girl. On bad days, when Xena was cranky and ungiving, I consoled myself with the thought that soon I would share the load with someone else. But every good day—and they had started to outnumber the bad—felt bittersweet. Xena and I had been a fairly exclusive couple for all of her life, but now I was conscious that our exclusive relationship was living on borrowed time.

Chapter 16

Six months—the *halfway mark*

By the time Xena was six months old, life had become much more pleasant—even though I didn't even notice it at first (which was ironic given that I had been holding out for better times since about, oh, day one after Xena's birth). Then again, it wasn't as though I was careening out of control one minute and cruising easy street the next; our return to civilised living was more of a gradual slide. The Big Guy and I patted each other on the back and chinked glasses every now and again, reflecting on our achievements thus far. We had survived the worst time, with its guaranteed broken nights and shattered days, emerging to discover a fairly peaceful existence.

Of course, everything is relative, and a rare 6.30 am wake-up call from Xena was now considered a luxurious morning sleep-in. Xena slept twice a day for anywhere between one and three hours, and crashed out for good between 6 pm and 7 pm at the end of the day. There was no longer any mystery about if and when she'd sleep, her tired signs becoming almost as familiar as my own. As soon as those fists started to work their way up to her eyes I'd scoop her up and put her to bed, where miraculously she would sleep. On the rare occasion when she did protest, a warm bottle or a quick walk around the block in her stroller would do the trick. And of course, if all else failed, there was always the car. On more than one occasion, I had guaranteed an easy transfer into her cot by synchronising a return trip home with her approximate sleeping time.

Our days were fragmented, structured as they were around Xena's sleeping times, but the upshot was well worth the minor limitations. We went out during her awake times and either slept or did our own thing at home while she napped. Compared to what we had been through, this felt like bliss.

Night-time was usually just as orderly and manageable, although we were still at risk of the odd night or three from hell when something bugged Xena and she in turn bugged us about it at the highly inappropriate time of 3 am or 4 am.

Night waking in older babies

It's not uncommon for babies aged between six and 12 months who have previously been sleeping well to start waking and calling for you during the night. Reasons for night waking at this age include:

- *separation anxiety.* This stage of development can occur any time from about six months and may cause your baby to cry out for you when he or she naturally wakes at night and discovers you aren't there.

- *mobility.* Your baby may travel around the cot at night and may bump awake, or

She'd been on solids as well as formula from four months of age, so I was pretty sure that any night waking wasn't due to hunger, but I'd usually end up feeding her anyway just to get her back to sleep. I'd quickly learnt that pacing the floor, rocking or patting her was fine as long as I was prepared to go through those motions all night long, but otherwise fairly useless, as she'd howl even louder as soon as I put her back down in her cot. A gently warmed bottle, on the other hand, (often with a side order of Panadol if I was confident she was teething) always soothed the savage beast. Well, almost always.

About the time Xena was approaching the age of seven months, there was an incident that will forever be known as Those 12 Nights of Hell.

We had put Xena to bed, as usual, at 6 pm, and then spent the evening watching an inane teeny-bopper movie that no self-respecting adult should be forced to endure—except

Midnight feasts

By six months of age, night waking probably isn't caused by hunger and many experts say that healthy babies of that age do not need night feeds for their health or growth. Having said that, if feeding your baby when he or she wakes at night helps him or her to go back to sleep and you don't mind the interruption, then go for it.

wake from cold if the coverings have been kicked off.

- *teething*. Teeth pushing their way through gums may make your baby sore and grumpy during the day or night.

- *nappy leak*. Cot bedding can get wet and cold if there has been a nappy leak and this can wake a sleeping bub.

- *illness*. Discomfort caused by a symptom of an illness may make bub unable to self-settle if he wakes throughout the night.

- *dummy dependence*. Bub may not be able to find the dummy, and could need your help with 're-plugging'.

in the privacy of their own homes where no-one can hear them cackle!—before hitting the sack a few hours later. At 1.30 am I was blasted from my sleep by Xena, who obviously had issues. Unperturbed, I lurched straight towards the kitchen to make and heat a small bottle, annoyed that I had been required to leave my nice warm bed, but knowing that I'd be back there in five or 10 minutes after the bottle had worked its magic. At least that was the plan. Xena scoffed the bottle, but instead of drifting off to sleep as she usually did, she decided to sit up, toss the bottle against the bars of the cot and howl. Houston, we had a problem. My never-fail settling method had failed and I wasn't at all sure what to try next. Teething gel for instant relief? Crying. Panadol for any unidentifiable pain? Still crying. Pacing and rocking? Crying.

Serious sleep issues

If night waking seems excessive and nothing you do helps, ask your GP or child health nurse for a referral to a local sleep clinic run by a reputable parenting organisation. 'Sleep school', as it's commonly referred to, has helped thousands of unhappy babies and parents rediscover the joys of deep, unbroken sleep.

After a while, the Big Guy dragged himself out of bed to enquire grumpily why I felt the need to torture my child at such an ungodly hour of the morning. 'I'm not *doing* anything', I hissed, by this time feeling desperately uneasy. What were we going to do? More formula, gel and Panadol weren't options for fairly obvious health reasons, which meant there was no choice but to rock and pat, rock and pat, pacing the floor in her room until my arms went numb, my back ached and Xena finally fell into an exhausted sleep. She did wake momentarily as I lowered her into her cot, but I leant over the bars and patted her all the way back to sleep. Then I inched my way out of her room, ever so slowly, taking care not to make the slightest noise. The entire back-breaking exercise took almost an hour and a half before I fell back into bed and slept like the dead until her cries woke me up again in the real morning.

Leaving babies to cry

Leaving babies to cry themselves to sleep is not advised for babies under six months of age. Most experts agree that babies this young cry because they are genuinely distressed or in need of help, not because they feel like being difficult. A recent theory suggests that ignoring a baby's cries only teaches bub not to seek or expect help.

After six months, a technique known as 'controlled crying' (also called controlled comforting or spaced soothing) can be used to teach babies to sleep. The technique, which is used by some sleep school practitioners, involves going to the baby when he or she cries out in the night, but leaving bub in the cot as you soothe him or her for a few minutes with words or gentle patting. You keep leaving and returning to soothe the baby in the same way, gradually increasing the minutes between visits, until bub goes back to sleep.

Not all experts (or parents) are fans of controlled crying. While some find it's the only way to teach an unsettled older baby to sleep, others argue that it's cruel and psychologically damaging to ignore a distressed baby.

All expert theory aside, if your sanity is in question due to lack of sleep and you want to give controlled crying a go, do so. Your mental health is important, too, and you need to be able to function as a parent. You can always stop if it doesn't feel right.

I wish I could say that was the end of the matter, but it wasn't. Xena did the same thing at the same time for eight more nights after that and, not for the first time in her short life, I almost went insane from lack of sleep. The Big Guy and I took turns repeating the same settling process every night, until finally we threw our hands up in defeat. When, on the tenth consecutive night, she let fly again neither the Big Guy nor I moved, except to put pillows over our heads. For an excruciatingly painful two hours we let her cry, holding each other back whenever resolve weakened. She did the same the following night, but her crying only lasted for about half an hour the night after that. On the thirteenth night, she slept through. The cause of her waking remained a complete mystery, but happily it never occurred again. From that day on, she really did always sleep through the night.

Early wakers

Let's face facts: some babies just go through a period of early waking and there's nothing you can do about it except grin, bear it and make sure you nap during the day and go to bed early at night to catch up on your own sleep. Having said that, it's always worth trying the following ideas to attempt to delay your baby's wake-up call to a more civilised hour:

- Invest in blockout blinds or curtains to keep bub's room as dark as possible.

- When you hear your baby waking up, leave bub for a few minutes to see if he or she settles back to sleep.

- Play some gentle, soothing music.

- Give bub a quiet feed and put him or her straight back down.

- Bring bub into your bed, where (hopefully) he or she will doze off with you.

- Put bub to bed a little later than normal. (Warning: this may work for some babies, but others will simply wake at the same time, feeling tired and grumpy.)

- Check that the last daytime nap is not too long or late in the day.

There was a trade-off for our guaranteed uninterrupted night's sleep, and that was Xena's preferred waking time of, gulp, 5 am. I can't recall exactly when this started to become the norm, but I can tell you that we weren't too happy about it. In our pre-baby days we had a rule: if the number on the clock started with a six, it was too early to get out of bed. Now we had a living alarm clock stuck permanently on five, and every now and again it went off 10 minutes earlier, which meant sometimes we began our day with a number that started with a *four*. Oh for a snooze button on that girl!

Physically getting out of bed was the hard part, but once we were actually up it wasn't too bad. Xena was usually pretty happy after 10 or 11 hours of sleep and all she wanted was a nice warm bottle of formula followed by play, which at her stage was fairly rudimentary. Picking up toys, shaking toys, gumming toys and then throwing toys down in disgust was about as interesting as it got unless we were prepared to be active at that ungodly hour and roll around tickling her or playing peek-a-boo. More often than not, we weren't up for the active option, preferring to nurse cup after cup of hot coffee while Xena sat at our feet and did her thing. Still, we did wish she would do her thing at a more socially acceptable hour.

Early to bed for early risers

If your baby wakes early (say 5 am–ish), but seems really tired by the end of the day, try putting bub to bed half an hour earlier at night. Going to bed over-tired may be the thing that's preventing him or her from sleeping through until a little later in the morning.

The days were long when they started so early, and often we'd be amazed to discover that even though Xena had drunk a bottle, eaten breakfast, played for an hour and enjoyed a 45-minute walk in the stroller, it was still only 7 am. I remembered a time when I had wished my weekends would pass by a little more slowly than they did. This was not what I'd had in mind.

Thankfully by about 7.30 am Xena was ready for her first nap of the day, rubbing her eyes and almost begging to be carried back into her room (which we happily did). Then it was back to sleep for a couple of hours for all of us. By the time we awoke for the second time that day—usually about 9 am—we'd feel much more refreshed, if not a little disoriented by our second wake-up of the day. Welcome to Groundhog Day...again.

The Big Guy and I did the caring sharing thing for about a month, and both got up to tend to Xena, before we realised the futility of both of us getting up so early. From that moment on we took turns. But while this was the fairest way of dividing the hard yards, it also divided the bedroom as we both defended our right to enjoy as much time in bed as was humanly possible. One of us defended our right more than the other...

Growing healthy habits

Gnawing on plain biscuits makes babies happy, but it's much better to get them used to snacking on fruit. Go to a baby store and look for a fresh food feeder to fill with soft fruit (or even vegetables and cooked meat) that bub safely sucks through a net. Messy and gross, yes, but well worth it to give bub a taste for healthy snacking.

Back at Fletch and Sarah's place one afternoon, after Xena's second and final nap for the day, we found ourselves sitting over a quiet beer. Ruby was toddling around the garden while Xena sat with us on a blanket under a tree, doing some serious damage to a Milk Arrowroot biscuit. She had learnt to sit up without help, and this had brought blessed relief to our household. Her new perspective of the world seemed to agree with her and she was now a much happier chappie—especially when Milk Arrowroot biscuits were involved. She'd sit happily and gum a bicky to within an inch of its life. The best thing about this was that it kept her amused for 15 minutes—30 if we doubled her ration (which we did more times than I'd care to admit).

Spring had well and truly sprung, and I was in a great mood. I waved happily at Xena and was rewarded with a big smile and a round of applause as she smashed her chubby palms together repeatedly.

'Hey Fletch,' I said, 'now this really is the life!'

Let me entertain you

Once your baby is sitting up and managing solids, you'll probably find that he or she will enjoy sitting around with other kids and grown-ups, and you can start to have a social life again (albeit a very different one from the pubbing and clubbing you experienced before being a parent). Just keep a few tricks up your sleeve to keep bub happily entertained for as long as possible when you want to sit outside with friends and enjoy the day. The following techniques can be really useful in keeping bub entertained and happy:

- *blowing bubbles.* You can buy bottles of bubble liquid and bubble blowers from two dollar shops or supermarkets. Keep a set in the nappy bag.

- *filling an old handbag with safe things.* Bub will have a great time taking the contents of the bag in and out, in and out ... you get the drift. Make sure you don't include anything smaller than a film canister, as this size item is a choking hazard for under threes.

- *hiding a few toys under a blanket.* Let your baby hunt for the toys, and give bub a big 'clap hands' when he or she finds them.

- *giving bub one sultana at a time to pick up off a plate and eat.* You'll be amazed how busy this keeps your baby.

Chapter 17

Get set for *back to work*

Six weeks before I was due back at work, I spotted a banner hanging across the fence of a day care centre I hadn't visited before. It was slightly out of our council's area, which is why it hadn't been on my list, but still close enough to home to be do-able. 'We're taking bookings', the banner screamed. '0–2 babies room. Caring environment. Hot lunch provided.' On impulse I drove into the driveway and went inside to speak to the manager. Thirty minutes later I emerged with a place for Xena secured. Good old blind faith. Something *had* turned up, and on the surface that something looked pretty good. Everything was coming together nicely.

I was starting to look forward to going back to work and running to my familiar professional timetable, as opposed to Xena's infantile routine. The thought of attacking work projects and seeing them completed had become vaguely enticing, more so than in my pre-baby days. Back then, work was work: a way of earning money in-between pastimes I really enjoyed. Now work beckoned as an interesting challenge, something a tad more stimulating than naps, nappies, dummies, dirty bums, feeding, fussing and playing goo goo ga ga on the floor.

I was ready to prove to myself that I hadn't gone brain dead after months of looking after my baby, as everyone had predicted.

But then Xena went and messed with my head by being the sweetest, happiest, sunniest little bubaloo I had ever seen.

The weekend before I was due back at work was one of the most pleasant weekends Xena and I'd had together. The Big Guy was away on a boys' weekend, so it was just us girls. We went visiting, sat in coffee shops (yes, it had finally happened!) and crawled around on a blanket under the shade of my favourite tree in the garden, laughing at Xena's comical reaction

The great day care debate

Everyone has an opinion about day care, and the loudest voices are usually the scariest, hammering home the message that 'all kids should be at home with mum, especially in the first few years'. But working mums are a fact of life, as is day care for working parents who can't afford a nanny or don't have a family who can help with child minding.

The truth is that research shows both positive and negative outcomes associated with babies attending day care, but the negatives get the most airtime because they generate sensational headlines and emotionally charged debate from working to her first-ever lick of ice-cream. If I hadn't been so busy being in love with my daughter, I would have been furious: how dare she suddenly become so much fun and so easy to look after when we were only a day or two away from being split up?

The Big Guy and I had decided to have a trial day care run for two days of each of the two weeks leading up to my return. With four days of freedom up my sleeve, I envisaged myself hitting the beach, having a massage or seeing a movie. Each suggestion was tantalising, as was the thought of time to myself. But first I had to deposit Xena at day care.

The drop-off started well enough, and I was relieved to see that Xena looked interested in the new surroundings and not at all shocked or upset. We sat down together on the floor, next to a baby in a rocker, while the teacher in charge of the room gathered some extra paperwork for me to take home and complete. The baby in the rocker looked about Xena's age. Xena, in turn, looked delighted to meet this new potential playmate and quickly rolled off

and non-working parents across all generations. Research demonstrating the benefits of day care doesn't pack the same punch, so it gets buried.

Put simply, it's not ideal for littlies to spend the entire week at day care if they are deposited at breakfast and reclaimed at bedtime because this restricts the opportunity for all-important one-on-one bonding with their parents. However, if working families spend quality time in the mornings, afternoons and weekends, or if attendance at day care can be limited to just a few days per week, your little one will get the best of both worlds: close contact with mum and dad, and the broader skills set and independence learned from day carers and other kids.

her bottom onto her hands and knees to crawl right up to her face. Rocker baby took one look at Xena, peering intently into her eyes—then promptly dropped her bottom lip and burst into tears. Xena's face registered complete shock for a split second before she joined in and, not long after, my face crumpled, too. In tears, I held my girl to my chest, rocking back and forth and wondering: how could I leave her? What if she became upset, like this other little one? Who would comfort *her*?

This was far too much pain to bear. I'd wanted to leave my baby and now I didn't want to leave her. I had longed for this day—the first day to myself in nine months—but now I wanted it to be over before it had even begun. I wanted to scoop up Xena, take her home, ring work to tell them I'd changed my mind and lock out the rest of the world while Xena and I soaked each other up. I'd let the Big Guy in, but no-one else, because no-one else loved her the way we did.

Do the sums

Before you commit to going back to work for financial reasons, calculate your after-tax income for the year, then deduct the following annual costs:

- *child care.* If you're entitled to a child care rebate or tax benefit, take that off your total.

- *travel expenses.* Be sure to include fares, tolls, petrol and mechanical services (which will occur more frequently if you are driving greater distances).

- *lunch and coffee.* You'll swear you'll take your lunch from home every day, but be realistic and assume you'll end up buying it half the time, plus you'll need coffee to get you through work days that follow broken nights.

The teacher returned to find us both crying and calmly but firmly extracted Xena from my arms and urged me to go home. 'Call any time you like', she said with the experience of scores of blubbering mums under her belt. 'She'll be fine. Do something nice for yourself today and we'll see you in the afternoon.'

Oh boy. Nobody had told me that leaving my child would be this hard. I'd heard about the morning rush to get to child care before work, watching the clock all day to get back to your child on time and how frantic life was as a working mum. No-one had mentioned how traumatic it would be to say goodbye, even when part of me was sure I was ready to say it. No-one talked about the incredible sadness or how you just can't stop the flood of tears, or how to handle the heartache. Not one word about how leaving my child would feel like the wrong thing to do; about how every bone in my body would scream at me to stop and reconsider. Sobbing all the way, I drove home—alone.

- *work clothing and shoes.* Nominate an amount for items you don't have but will need, such as a coat for winter. Bear in mind that you may need a whole new wardrobe for each season if your old work clothes no longer fit.

- *convenience foods/takeaway.* There will probably be at least one night a week when you are too tired to cook.

- *extra expenditure on convenience shopping.* Calculate the difference between buying nappies/formula/milk/bread at specialty shops rather than the supermarket at least once a week.

- *any other related expenses.*

If there is precious little money left over, you might want to reconsider your return to the workforce at this point. Just a thought.

It took one hour and an incomprehensible (on my side of the line) phone call to the Big Guy before I was calm. Well, I had stopped crying at least—although my heart was still racing, and would seize up every time I thought about my girl.

Wandering through the empty house I ended up in Xena's room, where her pyjamas lay on the floor by the change table, threatening to set me off again. Turning to leave, I was stopped by the sight of a crack in one of the walls that I hadn't had time to paint before she was born. Suddenly I knew how I would spend my day.

🍼 🍼 🍼

Actually, painting and decorating Xena's room took the better part of each and every one of the four days she was in care before I went back to work. Dropping her off on the second day was easier than it had been on the first day, and the third and fourth days were easier still, now that I was confident that Xena thoroughly enjoyed her days, which she spent eating, sleeping and playing happily with the other babies and young toddlers at the centre. By the fourth day I didn't even shed a tear, but hurried back home to continue my furious nesting. A tad late to nest, perhaps, given that most people get stuck into nursery decorating before the baby's born, but then again I didn't feel like most people anymore. Secretly I suspected my nursery makeover was my way of showing Xena that, even though I was leaving her to return to work, this room was where she belonged; the place where she was loved most. Either that or it was driven by guilt, pure and simple. I preferred my first thought.

The nursery looked spectacular; in fact, aside from Xena, it was the thing in our house I was most proud of. At the end of those first four days of care, I was relieved to see that Xena was still my sunny Xena. She hadn't changed at all. I, on the other hand, was about to.

Leaving your baby with carers

Your baby will quickly get used to being left at day care for a while when he or she realises that mummy or daddy will always come back. To make the transition to child care easier for both of you, try the following tricks:

- Practise being apart from your baby for shorter bursts of time before leaving him or her for the whole day.

- Be positive when you drop your baby off at day care, as this conveys a message that he or she is in a safe, happy place.

- If your baby cries when you go to leave, remain calm, give bub a kiss and cuddle goodbye, and hand over to one of the carers.

- Never sneak out or leave without saying goodbye, even if bub is upset. This will make your little one more anxious and distrustful of the whole situation.

- Be positive and happy, as opposed to apologetic or overly clingy, when you return, to send the message that day care is a good place.

- Establish a good relationship with the carer/s at the childcare centre. They can keep you up to date with what bub is doing during the day, and how he or she is coping with the change.

- Find out the correct procedure for raising concerns with the centre, and always address anything that's bothering you rather than stewing over something you have seen or heard.

Chapter 18

The business of being a *working mum*

Going back to work turned my life upside down—yet again. Sometimes I felt sad that I didn't know what my baby was doing during the day—whether she was happy, unhappy, sleeping, awake or attempting to take her first steps. The carers at day care were very considerate, and would tell me that she either 'had a great day' or 'was a bit unsettled'. By that time I'd lived with Xena for long enough to know that the latter comment meant she had grizzled all day. Sheepishly I realised that I wasn't sorry to have missed those unsettled days when nothing could soothe my savage little beastie.

But most of the time Xena was as happy as the Big Guy and I were about our new routine. I was responsible for looking after Xena in the mornings, so I would get up and spend an early morning with Xena before taking her to the centre. The Big Guy took over at the end of the day, picking up Xena in the afternoon and taking her home for an early dinner and bath. If only I'd had the sense to delegate some of the Xena duties earlier on, we may all have been much happier much faster. The Big Guy thrived in his new role as a hands-on dad, relishing the opportunity to get to know his daughter without his pesky wife standing over him and sighing that he was 'doing it all wrong and let me do that for you, dear'.

Cover up

After you get dressed for work in the morning, pop your dressing gown (or one of your partner's old business shirts) over your outfit so you can pick up your little one without worrying about grotty little hands messing you up. Just don't forget to de-robe before you leave the house!

If anyone asked me—and they did, frequently—'How do you do it?' my answer would vary, depending on whether I was tired from broken sleep,

Sanity savers for working mums

The trick to being a working mum is keeping everyone fed, clean, clothed and where they need to be, when they need to be there. Here are a few tips many working mums swear by:

- *embrace bulk buying and bulk cooking*. Spend an hour on the weekend listening to music while you cook and freeze a few meals for the week ahead.

- *discover slow cookers*. Fill a slow cooker with meat or vegetables and sauce in the morning, and come home to a beautifully tender meal that's ready to eat.

- *lower your standards*. Toasted sandwiches, canned soup and baked beans all count as meals.

- *think ahead*. Pack everything you need for the next day at night, and place by the door.

racked with guilt because I was missing Xena or feeling invincible because work and home were running like clockwork. The most difficult times were when Xena was sick, because I couldn't bear to leave her. On those days I didn't try too hard to find a stand-in babysitter, instead taking the day off to look after her myself (even though I would then feel guilty about letting people down at work). The other option was to let Xena down when she needed me, which wasn't really an option at all. On such days I put everything on hold and stayed with Xena until she was well again, knowing that I'd have to play catch up at work for days afterwards. It seemed a small price to pay to be with my girl when she needed me.

The grass isn't greener

Just quietly, I think that working mums and stay-at-home mums all envy each other's perceived freedoms, although they'd be hard-pressed to admit it. The truth is that both options are a really tough gig. Embrace the gig you choose and, if it makes you miserable, think about what needs to change —then make it happen.

- *shop wisely when buying work clothes.* Buy mix and match work clothes that don't need ironing.

- *set up your car for split duties.* Get two car seats if you share the dropping-off and picking-up duties.

- *share chores with your partner.* Divvy up bill paying, shopping and laundry duties necessary during the week with your partner so one person doesn't cop it all.

- *Enlist a back-up person.* Arrange to have a reliable and trustworthy friend or family member that you can call on to pick up or care for your bub in emergencies.

- *factor in family down time.* Every weekend make sure there are a few scheduled hours when you, your partner and baby all just hang out doing nothing.

The other times when being a working mum was particularly tough were the days when Xena was asleep by the time I arrived home. On those nights, I'd usually burst into tears and let the Big Guy console me with a recount of her day and their afternoon. Sometimes this made me feel better, sometimes worse, depending on what I had missed and how desperately I had missed her.

As the weeks and months went by (once time crawled, now it flew!), Xena appeared to swing easily from home to day care and day care to home again. She enjoyed being part of a bigger group of children by all accounts, learning their names and blowing kisses to her favourite friends and teachers when we came and went to and from the centre. And home life became one big fun-fest: although our time together as a family was less in quantity, it increased in quality. I held Xena for longer and loved her harder than ever before.

On a fairly average day, my schedule ran something like this:

The night before a work day

Fall into bed before running through mental checklist. Bag packed? Check. Xena's bag packed? Check. Including dummies? Check. And blanky? Check (she'll be fine, stop worrying). Outfit ironed? Check. Xena already wearing tomorrow's outfit to save valuable time in morning? Check. Now shut up and get some sleep.

Still the night before the same work day

Become conscious of baby crying, realise baby is mine, stagger from bed to investigate cause. Check baby and sheets for signs of nappy leakage. Realise nappy has leaked, change baby out of outfit put on to save time in morning and make mental note that the Big Guy will pay for this.

And again, the night before the work day

Become conscious of baby crying again, realise baby is mine again, stagger from bed again to investigate. Feel baby's mouth to check for dummy. Realise dummy has escaped, search under cot for dummy and make mental note to wean baby from dummy sometime soon because this can't go on forever.

5.11 am Xena awake. Make warm bottle, kiss Xena's warm head repeatedly while feeding and try to open both eyes fully, at same time.

5.23 am Wait for big milk chuck that's bound to happen after Xena downs entire bottle without a break and crawls around floor to locate favourite toy: the remote control.

5.24 am Run to kitchen for paper towels and carpet cleaner. Note that both eyes are now fully opened, at same time.

5.32 am Play peek-a-boo with Xena and remote.

6.00 am Deposit Xena in bed with the Big Guy while I shower and dress. Listen to sounds of raucous tickle game while patting obscenely expensive anti-puff eye cream on obscenely puffy eyelids.

6.07 am Check puff has reduced enough to 'sweep light shimmering eye shadow over lids to create youthful, fresh appearance', just like fashion magazines told me.

6.08 am Decide to cancel fashion mag subscription and stick to parenting magazines.

6.23 am Reclaim Xena from the Big Guy (aka tickle monster) avoiding contact between Xena's drool-covered mouth and my freshly ironed shirt.

6.30 am Feed cereal to Xena with one hand while eating own breakfast with other. Resist all temptation to give Xena control of spoon, even though she's begging for it.

6.40 am Spend 10 minutes wiping cereal off Xena's head, face, hands, elbows and forearms before lifting her out of her highchair.

6.41 am Set her down and realise I've missed a spot, which is now mashed onto me. Head to laundry basket to find clean top that matches pants. Iron new top and remind myself to avoid picking up Xena for rest of morning.

7.00 am Have third coffee with the Big Guy and laugh as Xena attempts to eat remote and change channels simultaneously. Marvel how clever she is to find cartoons.

7.03 am Discover remote control is highly inappropriate toy after battery choking scare.

7.05 am Breathe sigh of relief that the 'hold her upside down and thump her back' manoeuvre works so well and find safe replacement toy for Xena.

7.15 am Protest indignantly, 'No, Big Guy, it wasn't me, but it could be Xena's nappy'.

7.16 am Wait for the Big Guy's offer to change offending nappy.

7.18 am Change the bloody nappy myself.

7.30 am Kiss the Big Guy goodbye and strap Xena into car seat, hoping she's over annoying phase of arching back and refusing to yield to seat. Drive to day care pointing out trains ('Look! Thomas!'), dogs ('Look! Woof woof!') and have several near misses at lights because I've been preoccupied with pointing out trains and dogs.

7.40 am Arrive at day care and spend 10 minutes crawling around with Xena while she 'settles in'. Pretend I don't know everyone at the centre thinks I'm over-protective and clingy.

7.50 am Realise 10 minutes of play may cost me my train unless I bolt. Try hard not to speed (too much) to get to station, and try hard not to slip (again) as I hurtle up stairs and onto platform to squeeze onto train just before doors close.

8.05 am Stand up on the train the entire way into town because there are no seats, but don't care because it's better than being nine months' pregnant and standing entire way into town.

8.59 am (if I'm lucky, but closer to 9.08 am on most days) Attempt to convey impression I've been at work for hours even though have just snuck in. Wonder how long I'll last before seeking audience for latest funny anecdote about Xena.

9.15 am Make 'to do' list for the day. Fight rising sense of panic after identifying 29 tasks to complete in eight hours, not including own personal 'to do at lunchtime' list.

9.20 am Start ploughing through work list, choosing easiest tasks first.

9.38 am Tick off three tasks and enjoy smug feeling of achievement.

9.42 am Interrupted by phone call from day care—Xena's feverish. Tell them 'someone' is on their way.

9.44 am Dial the Big Guy's mobile. No answer. Leave complicated message outlining problem and 17 possible solutions. Dial mother-in-law. Leave complicated message outlining her potential role in eight out of 17 emergency care plans. Dial the Big Guy's mobile again. Still no answer so nominate myself as 'someone'. Start packing up while rehearsing exit speech to boss.

9.48 am Interrupted by phone call from day care—false alarm. Xena fine, battery-operated thermometer very sick.

9.50 am Dial the Big Guy's mobile and mother-in-law leaving refreshingly simple messages. All's well, everybody stay put.

9.52 am Unpack bag and return to 'to do' list.

9.53 am Phone rings but too scared to answer in case it's day care again. Pick up phone gingerly and breathe sigh of relief. Only the boss.

10.27 am Tick off task seven and reward self with coffee and muffin break. Ignore fact that coffee man doesn't give two hoots about my child and show him latest photo anyway.

10.31 am Quick call to day care to check Xena really is okay.

11.00 am Meeting with important industry contact. Shake smooth, manicured hand with own rough detergent-ravaged hand. Decide to either get dishwasher or wean Xena off bottles asap.

11.50 am Run into Sam from accounts at photocopier on way back from meeting. Bail her up with quick story about Xena. Laugh uproariously at equally funny story about Sam's kid. Scatter at first sight of boss striding through office.

12.00 pm Return to 'to do' list.

12.30 pm Politely reject office junior's offer to get sandwiches. Sorely tempted to request sandwich run via chemist for nappies, but chicken out at last minute.

12.34 pm Address task 13.

12.58 pm Quick call from the Big Guy asking me to double-check on Xena. Dissuade him from making me call for third time, on grounds that Xena will be sleeping, although real reason is to avoid being labelled neurotic by day care teachers.

1.03 pm Oh what the heck, what's a little neurosis between friends? Call day care to check on Xena. She's fine and sleeping peacefully.

1.07 pm Lunch break, but first visit two ATMs before finding one that works. Shut eyes and hope fervently for enough money to cover two overdue bills and nappies. Phew, just! Stand in line at post office for 12 minutes to pay stupid bills. Buy nappies, baby Panadol, wipes and extra dummy at chemist. On impulse, decide to duck into supermarket and wait for seven minutes to pay for pumpkin, potatoes, rusks and baby custard. Discover exactly $4.70 left from $400 and kick myself for buying nappies and wipes at overpriced chemist instead of cut-price grocery chain. Head back to office, stopping at cheapest sandwich shop to buy overpriced salad sandwich and vow darkly to bring my lunch from home from now on.

1.58 pm Scoff salad sandwich at desk before returning to 'to do' list. Respond brightly to comments from colleagues who sat in park for lunch break. 'Was it really the most beautiful summer's day in the history of the civilised world? How lovely!' Pat self on back for demonstrating selfless ability to share other people's joy when actually I am jealous as all hell.

2.00 pm Return to 'to do' list and calculate time remaining to complete last 12 tasks. Two hundred and two minutes divided by 12 is approximately 16 minutes for each task.

2.41 pm Called into boss's office. Hope it's not about earlier conversation at photocopier with Sam in accounts.

2.46 pm Leave boss's office with three extra tasks to add to today's list. Calculate time remaining and hope for miracle.

2.47 pm Head down, bum up. Ignore conversation about last night's episode of *Masterchef* even though I am dying to know who won. Who on earth wants to eat cubic squid ink noodles, anyway?

2.48 pm Tell office junior to come back on payday for donation to baby shower gift for Sue-Ellen in publicity because am broke. Hear single girls give same excuse. Resist urge to write what I really want to say ('Are you *sure* you want to do this?') and sign card with benign prattle about best wishes for new arrival instead.

2.49 pm Head down, bum up.

3.49 pm   Yikes! Nearly forgot to make doctor's appointment for Xena's immunisation/rash/red eye/cough or latest worrisome condition of the week. Phone doctor and make Saturday appointment for third week in a row.

3.50 pm   Head down, bum up.

4.27 pm   Big Guy calls for grocery update. Give him list of things I forgot to get at lunch. Hear Xena chortling in background and ache to feel her weight on my hip.

4.32 pm   Six tasks to go. Feel adrenalin rising. Wait! That's not adrenalin, just haven't been to toilet all day. Hurry to bathroom.

4.34 pm   Am reminded of need to close toilet door after embarrassing incident with Jenny from advertising. Apologise profusely and race back to desk, hoping fire in cheeks will subside.

4.35 pm   Ring Jenny to reiterate that I am not a pervert, I am just a mum who's become accustomed to leaving toilet doors wide open out of necessity.

4.38 pm   Hang up and convince self that howls of laughter from Jenny's office have nothing to do with me.

4.39 pm   Head down, bum up. Five tasks remaining.

4.45 pm   Four.

5.00 pm   Three.

5.15 pm   Two.

5.20 pm   Decide last two tasks can wait until tomorrow. Pack up in record time, grabbing nappies, groceries and work file to read on way home on the train.

5.22 pm   Hope no-one notices I left eight minutes early, but forced to take gamble because later train means 20 minutes less of Xena. And that's just not on.

5.25 pm Try hard not to slip (again) as I hurtle up stairs and onto platform to squeeze onto train just before doors close. Stand entire way home because there are no seats, but don't care because it's better than being nine months' pregnant and standing entire way home.

6.15 pm Skid into driveway, wrench up handbrake and burst through front door. Fast-paced, time-focused world stops at exact moment of laying eyes on Xena. Eat her up with kisses.

6.17 pm 'Ah, there you are Big Guy. How ya doing?'

Yep, all up, just your fairly average day.

Chapter 19

Home, *safe home*

It had been a long time between newspapers, but finally one Sunday morning Xena presented me with the ultimate gift of a few moments of my own time to flick through the tabloids while she played at my side. Judging by the happy babbling and delighted squeals, she was having a ball crawling around on the floor, diligently ignoring the multitude of educationally sound toys in favour of tasting stray breadcrumbs, dried peas, dead flies and numerous other health hazards that I probably shouldn't be admitting to.

Thoroughly enjoying the indulgence of daytime reading while Xena was awake, I made my way to the lifestyle section of the magazine lift-out. This used to be my favourite section of the mag, back in the days when redecorating was something I did for enjoyment, rather than out of necessity. My most inspired creative moments had since regressed to finding new corners of the kitchen bench to stack up sterilised bottles and disguising milk-vomit stains on the carpet by artfully repositioning the play gym.

The house featured in the lifestyle section that week was rather stunning, and was home to a couple of cute curly headed moppets (who looked as though they'd stepped out of the latest Pumpkin Patch catalogue) and their equally stylish parents. To describe the home as tasteful would have been an understatement. In contrast, our home since Xena's arrival could best be described as 'tasty' given the amount of foodstuffs that had since found their way onto our couches, walls, carpet and random pieces of furniture. After nine months of domestic chaos, picture-perfect households such as these were about as achievable as a sleep-in till nine in the morning. They also disproved my theory that motherhood and a messy home went hand-in-hand, which was a major inconvenience and meant I'd either have to hide the article or think up a new excuse to tell the Big Guy.

Making your home baby-friendly

As soon as your baby shows signs of intent to crawl, it's time to baby-proof your home. Most safety experts recommend that parents crawl around each room and eyeball what your baby will soon be eyeballing. Is it dangerous? If so, cover it up, remove it or fix it so it's safe. When baby-proofing your home, make sure you do the following things:

- Secure any furniture that can be pulled down onto a child (such as flat-pack bookshelves and big-screen TVs) to the wall.

- Remove dangerous items and poisonous chemicals (that is, bathroom or kitchen products, alcohol, glass and sharp things) from low cupboards, or install childproof locks on cupboards.

- Ensure blind cords are out of reach in all rooms and away from baby's cot.

- Drain buckets, eskies and paddling pools after use, and ensure that pool fences meet safety standards and are kept closed. Keep ponds covered with a fixed grill.

- Block off stairs and no-go zones, such as fireplaces, heaters, electrical outlets and power boards.

- Cover any really sharp furniture edges, especially coffee tables, with corner protectors.

- Check window screens can't be pushed out by little hands.

- Supervise your baby around pets, and use a safety gate to keep pets out of baby's bedroom.

- Use a bath thermometer to ensure bath water doesn't exceed 37 degrees, keep hot cups of coffee and tea out of reach, and turn handles of pots on the stove inwards to reduce accidental burns and scalds.

- Never assume you can pour boiled water or drink hot drinks safely with an infant in your arms.

By the end of the piece I wanted to throw the gagging gesture at Mr and Mrs Perfect, with their immaculate house and equally immaculate offspring. Xena herself was gagging on her latest find—a long-lost dirt-encrusted rusk. As I plucked the offending object out of her mouth with my dribble-covered fingers, I reflected on the other changes to my life since Xena's arrival.

The first thing that struck me—quite possibly because Xena had started bouncing up and down on my lower abdomen—was that I no longer peed in private. The bathroom door was always wide open, and I was usually accompanied by Xena either in a bouncer, on my lap or crawling around my legs while I completed my, ahem, business.

And speaking of privacy, I'd lost all sense of body-related shyness. A Pap smear no longer filled me with dread, purely because it seemed like the whole world had seen my most intimate bits anyway.

My body had actually borne the brunt of a whole lot of changes, I mused, carrying Xena into the kitchen to fix a snack while trying my best to ignore the sharp pain resonating from my lower back. Aside from being able to function—just—on five or six hours sleep instead of the eight to 10 hours I used to need, I also walked with a permanent crook in my back caused by Xena's Preferred Hip Syndrome. But it wasn't all bad news. XPHS had also prompted me to master the art of cooking, cleaning and blow-drying my hair while toting said baby on said hip, which was an achievement of sorts as long as you didn't look too closely at the back of my head.

My bodgy hairdo might have been of more concern had the Big Guy and I started rubbing shoulders with the A-list crowd, but as it was our social life had undergone a makeover, too, and we were now hanging out with the ABC for Kids set. Restaurants, pubs and clubs had been replaced with backyards, parks and food halls. I used to sneer at the shopping centre food hall, thinking it had nothing to offer me and my up-market tastes. Well, up-market went downmarket quite frequently nowadays, especially when there was a need for a nearby parents' room to warm a bottle or change a dirty nappy.

Aside from being a food hall snob, I'd also been a movie snob, generally choosing to bypass the latest blockbuster out of a steady refusal to watch mainstream trash. Now I'd happily cop an eyeful of Tom, Brad or any other pretty boy marketed at people like me who don't get out much.

Once upon a time I had gone out with friends for sushi, catching up with who'd done what, where and how. Now I went out with Xena and the Big Guy for hot chips, catching up with other families just like us.

So, did I miss my up-market predilections in entertainment and home decorating? No, I decided, as Xena reached out and knocked over the glass of juice I had just poured myself, having the perfect home no longer interested me. Of much greater concern were the people who lived in my home, and that was perhaps the most significant life change of all.

Chapter 20

Happy *first* *birthday*, baby

It was a mild autumn night and the Big Guy and I were lying in bed talking about stuff. Nothing exciting—just Xena, bills, Xena, how broke we were, Xena, how exhausted we were, Xena, how we didn't know where the past year had gone, Xena...

'Hard to believe she's nearly one', I said sleepily. 'Where's our baby gone?'

'Hopefully she's gone to sleep,' the Big Guy muttered, 'and hopefully you'll stop yapping so I can go to sleep, too'.

'I know, let's throw a party for her', I enthused, completely ignoring his plea for peace. 'Nothing big, just a few friends and family.'

'Fine, as long as you promise me you won't go over the top', the Big Guy acquiesced, before burying his head under a pillow. 'Just remember how broke we are.' Now what made him think I'd go over the top? Xena was only turning one after all. It wasn't like it was her 21st.

🐧🐧🐧

Two weeks, 17 hours of preparation and two packets of *Bananas in Pyjamas* invitations later, I was putting the final touches on a metre-long B1 cake, hanging the last of the 50 Bananas-themed balloons, sprinkling hundreds and thousands on an entire loaf of sliced buttered bread and wondering what had made me think we could accommodate 23 adults and 19 children ranging from three months to 13 years in the shoebox we called home. I hoped the hired clown wouldn't be late.

When our first guests arrived, Xena was sound asleep, having spent an exhausting (for me!) morning chasing balloons, shrieking like a banshee when they burst in her face and howling indignantly when, fearful of the potential choke factor, I removed the shreds of rubber from her clutches. The well-used sign on the front door 'Quiet please, baby sleeping' directed people straight around to the backyard, to avoid waking the guest of honour.

I made good use of Xena's final few minutes of sleep to heat the hot snacks, serve the cold drinks and bribe the older children with gratuitous gifts of lollies that I would never allow my own child to eat. By the time she woke — hot, groggy and crumpled — there were 42 people bursting to greet the birthday girl, who took one look at the sea of beaming expectant faces and collapsed in a screaming heap. No amount of 'Look, there's Grandma!' or 'Say hi to Aunty JoJo' could turn that pitiful frown upside down. Even our never-fail back-up plan of a horsey ride on Daddy's leg could not shake away the tears.

Farewell baby, hello toddler!

Congratulations! After 12 months, your baby is officially considered a toddler. This means:

- formula is no longer required

- breastfeeding can stop or continue, as you please

- sterilising bottles and dummies (if indeed you have been doing this all along) can stop

- cows' milk can become bub's main drink, supplemented with water in between if needed

- bottles can be replaced with sipper cups or cups with straws

- baby purees can be taken off the menu and you can move bub onto mashed or chopped-up family meals

- being hand-fed may no longer interest your baby, and he or she may want to take over this job herself—so be prepared for mess!

- daytime sleeps may be cut down to one a day, although bub may still need two from time to time

- language skills might be starting to develop—bub may understand the meaning of several words, and be able to say a few, too

- bub may become more assertive about what he or she does and doesn't want to do—so get your boundaries and strategies in place now, including what is and isn't permitted in your home, and how to react to tantrums and undesirable behaviour.

Given Xena's dire need to meld herself into my body, I had no choice but to hoist her up on my hip, with her legs locked firmly around my waist and her face mashed into my collarbone. Thus joined, we embarked on umpteen return trips from the kitchen to the backyard, bringing out plate upon plate of sausage rolls, mini meatballs, nachos, pasties and hot chips. Pretending I couldn't see the Big Guy gesturing that we had enough greasy food to last until Xena's next birthday, I made one last visit to the kitchen to heat up the 'little boys'.

With the final food-related chore completed, Xena and I rejoined our guests who, by now, had raised a rousing call for 'pressie time'. Plonking myself on a square inch of floor that wasn't occupied by toddlers, babies, half-eaten jelly beans and slops of nachos, I plonked Xena on my lap and let the fun and games begin.

Pressie time ended up being a real hit, even if the actual gifts themselves were almost completely redundant. The designer clothes, dolls with bottles (what, no breastfeeding?) and aggravatingly noisy toys lay discarded. Of more interest to Xena — as soon as she had recovered from the fright of a singing and dancing Elmo — was the colourful wrapping paper and her newly discovered ability to pulp. And speaking of masticating cardboard — the cocktail frankfurts!

Racing back into the kitchen I discovered the distraction of pressie time had cost our little boys their bright red skins, which now resembled a mass of swirling ribbons floating among the overcooked franks. Salvageable? Just. I dumped the lot of them on a platter with the obligatory bowl of tomato sauce in the middle and, stepping over the eight older children who were trying to fit under Xena's playgym at the same time, made one last deposit on the table, which was groaning with the weight of too much food. Finally, I flopped down next to my mum, but I still had a feeling I'd forgotten something.

Xena! Where was she?

The Big Guy looked up from the chicken nibblies he was cooking on the barbecue when, in a panic, I asked him where our daughter was. 'I thought she was with you.'

'Who's got Xena?' I jumped up, yelling frantically over the cacophony of Wiggles music, children yelping and raucous laughter from the 'big people' getting into the champagne I hadn't had a chance to touch. Oh crikey, I'd only had her for a year and already I'd lost her.

'She's under the table', yelled Xena's seven-year-old cousin Jack, before he dived back into the fray under the play gym. 'Oh thank goodness', I sighed, as 21 pairs of eyes peered under the table to discover my daughter happily gnawing away on an object she'd obviously found in one of our guests' handbags, the contents of which had been tipped upside down on her lap.

But hang on — what was that all over her hands and down the side of her face?

'BLOOD!' I screeched in horror. 'Oh my God, she's BLEEDING!'

The Big Guy dropped his tongs and bolted towards us while our guests scrambled up to help, and I commando rolled under the table to disarm Xena and begin the process of administering first aid. Despite her obvious flesh wounds, she was remarkably calm. Smiling even. I, on the other hand, had to fight back the urge to faint. 'Oh, my brave darling', I murmured, scooping her up and searching tentatively for the actual wound under all the blood. But hang on, that wasn't blood, it was … a sickening mixture of drool and lipstick. Xena held up her 'weapon' triumphantly. 'Nyum nyum nyum.'

Swiftly replacing the half-chewed lippie with a conveniently self-skinned frank, I left Xena happily munching away and attempted to restore order in the house with a well-timed bite to eat. 'Little boys, anyone? Cocktail frankfurts?'

Where the hell was that damn clown?

When the exact moment of the anniversary of Xena's birth arrived, I sought out the Big Guy for a cuddle. Xena had since acclimatised to the crowd and was enjoying her choice of laps—birthday girl or not, she never wanted for a set of arms when the family was around.

'Hey, Big Guy, we've made it', I snuggled into his shoulder, marvelling at how I could become so distracted by the physical presence of my daughter that I often overlooked the physical presence of my husband. Without him, there would have been no Xena, but without Xena there would still be him.

I vowed silently never to take him for granted again. Out loud, I apologised for being such a Jekyll and Hyde for the past 12 months. 'I don't know if you really know this,' I confessed, 'but I really struggled with being a parent, and sometimes even wanted to turn back the clock. Do you know what I'm talking about?' He nodded, before planting a deliberately long, hard kiss on my lips. 'Matey, you've done a great job but you still have a big lesson to learn. Despite what you may think, you were never alone. Maybe next time you'll let me play a bigger role than just your support act.'

He was right, of course—I'd overlooked my biggest ally and greatest supporter when he'd been there all along, just waiting for me to ask for his help. Had I not been so caught up with doing everything myself, I could have made both of our lives a lot less complicated and a lot more entwined.

But hang on one second—did he just say 'next time'? The Big Guy looked at me and grinned.

Two days ago, with a frightfully overdue period nowhere to be seen, another pregnancy had seemed like the worst thing that could happen. Since then my body had told me not to expect a new life in the next nine months. I'd been shocked to find myself alternating between relief and disappointment.

The Big Guy's words were strangely comforting. Maybe next time would be different. I guess we'd just have to wait and see.

Postscript: staying mum

To all those people who patted my unborn baby through my bump, asking 'Is this your first? How lovely!' I have a question: why the code of silence? You had children in tow or at school — maybe even in remand centres — at the time of patting, and yet you still didn't tell me the truth. And to all those people who told me that a baby would just fit into my life perfectly, I had another question: Were you still sucking on gas at the time?

My baby changed, as opposed to fitted into, my life from the very first moment we met. And there was nothing 'lovely' about feeling so tired you could throw up, or struggling to attach a tiny mouth to enormous breasts in exactly the right position to fill a marble-sized belly for about two hours before having to go through the whole debacle all over again. My time had flown out the window, closely followed by my love life. And day by day I found myself wondering how a never-ending mountain of dirty laundry and endless trips to the baby aisle of the supermarket fitted in with being a 20-something career woman with an interesting life.

At 2 am one morning as I staggered up to tend to my wailing child while mulling over the work day ahead, I vowed that I would set the rest of the female population straight. And I knew exactly what I needed to tell them.

I'd start gently, by hinting that once they became a mother they may never again be seen with a cleaned and pressed outfit, a 'just stepped out of the salon' hairdo and an impeccably made-up face ... all at the same time. Then I'd tell them to throw their clock out the window because a) they would always run late, b) time would stand still and c) they wouldn't register the difference between night and day for many months anyway. The old saying 'time flies when you're having fun' did not apply to whole days left alone tending to a newborn, and it definitely wouldn't apply to the nights. It had no relevance whatsoever to the working mum's whirlwind schedule.

Then I'd get tough. Kiss your significant other goodbye, I'd say, trying to keep the sobs from rising up into my voice, because you won't want him to touch you for many months post-birth. When you finally relent you'll be too busy worrying how much precious sleep time you have sacrificed for the sake of a roll in the hay to be able to enjoy yourself.

You will be puked on and weed on from now until your child reaches school—and possibly beyond, I'd continue mercilessly. Get used to it. On occasions when *you* need to puke or wee, you will have to do so while still tending to your baby, because privacy and sick days are a thing of the past.

Sleep deprivation really, *really* hurts, I'd mutter darkly. More than labour, because it lasts longer — sometimes for years.

And, finally, the cold hard truth: you know all those Mother's Day ads? They lied. Having a baby isn't the blissful, peaceful, Madonna-esque existence we'd been led to believe. Sometimes you might feel like you have made a terrible mistake by bringing a child into the world; that you are not strong enough, selfless enough and capable enough to cope with one day, let alone one year or one lifetime, of being a mother. But that's not the worst thing. The worst thing is that the guilt of thinking that way about the tiny, helpless, innocent child that you also love more than life itself would just about cripple you.

🐝🐝🐝

My first chance to set the record straight came when a casual acquaintance rang to start spreading her news. Laura was 12 weeks and three days pregnant, but who was counting? Actually, she was, with that breathless excitement I remembered so well from my own 40-week countdown to Xena.

As Laura happily babbled on about the due date, morning sickness and how she just couldn't wait to meet the face behind the first grainy ultrasound image, I wondered what to mention first. The pain? The fatigue? The guilt?

Her next question — 'What's labour really like?' — provided the perfect starting point. I'd begin with a no-holds-barred view of birth, moving on to a sentiment-free account of breastfeeding and life with a newborn baby. As I geared up to offer some carefully chosen words of wisdom, Laura continued her chatter. 'I'm seriously considering using massage and heat packs for pain relief,' she bubbled, 'and the hospital said we were welcome to bring in music and games and cards and ...'

The mention of selecting music for the labour ward brought everything flooding back. My own excitement. The anticipation. My belief in myself. Had someone sat me down and told me what I wanted to say to Laura, what I was about to say to Laura, would they have helped or hindered me? Would I have accepted their experience of birth and motherhood as my benchmark?

As hard as it was to admit, I had to concede that my experience was mine alone. With her own baby on the way, the last thing Laura needed was to take on my own issues or to be influenced by my perception of the way birth and motherhood should, could or would be. She'd just have to get her own issues and hang-ups like the rest of us.

When I finally got a word in edgewise, I said the only thing there was left to say.

'This is your first baby, isn't it Laura? How lovely!'

Index